Church at Church

Church at Church

Jean-Jacques von Allmen's Liturgical Ecclesiology

by RONALD ANDREW RIENSTRA

PICKWICK *Publications* · Eugene, Oregon

CHURCH AT CHURCH
Jean-Jacques von Allmen's Liturgical Ecclesiology

Copyright © 2019 Ronald Andrew Rienstra. All rights reserved. Except for brief quotations in critical publications or reviews, no part of this book may be reproduced in any manner without prior written permission from the publisher. Write: Permissions, Wipf and Stock Publishers, 199 W. 8th Ave., Suite 3, Eugene, OR 97401.

Pickwick Publications
An Imprint of Wipf and Stock Publishers
199 W. 8th Ave., Suite 3
Eugene, OR 97401

www.wipfandstock.com

PAPERBACK ISBN: 978-1-5326-5182-3
HARDCOVER ISBN: 978-1-5326-5183-0
EBOOK ISBN: 978-1-5326-5184-7

Cataloging-in-Publication data:

Names: Rienstra, Ronald, Andrew, author

Title: Church at church : Jean-Jacques von Allmen's liturgical ecclesiology / by Ronald Andrew Rienstra.

Description: Eugene, OR : Pickwick Publications, 2019 | Includes bibliographical references.

Identifiers: ISBN 978-1-5326-5182-3 (paperback) | ISBN 978-1-5326-5183-0 (hardcover) | ISBN 978-1-5326-5184-7 (ebook)

Subjects: LCSH: Allmen, Jean-Jacques von, 1917–. | Worship. | Church. | Liturgics.

Classification: LCC BV600.2 R4 2019 (print) | LCC BV600.2 (ebook)

Manufactured in the U.S.A.   02/07/19

To Debra

Contents

Acknowledgments

I AM DEEPLY GRATEFUL to the following people:

- To Leanne VanDyk, Tim Brown, and my colleagues and friends at Western Theological Seminary, for their patience, encouragement, and faith.
- To Caitlin Johnson and Rita Selles, for help with translations from the French.
- To Brian Madison, whose research assistance was invaluable.
- To John Witvliet for friendship and inspiration.
- To Todd Johnson and Clay Schmit for wisdom and trust.
- To Debra and Miriam and Jacob and Philip, for support and forbearance.

Introduction

The meeting for worship is the church becoming church.

—GORDON LATHROP[1]

THE CRYSTAL CATHEDRAL: A CASE STUDY IN CONFUSED ECCLESIOLOGY

THE CRYSTAL CATHEDRAL CHURCH—or rather, the Christian ministry housed in the Crystal Cathedral of Garden Grove, California—went bankrupt in 2010. The landmark sanctuary and campus, an architectural expression of Protestantism, modernism, and post-modern consumer capitalism, was ordered by the court to be sold. A bid from Chapman University to turn the campus into a center for medical education was appealing, but the church's board of directors supported a bid from the Roman Catholic Diocese of Orange County instead.[2] In the news reports published in the days following the court order, contemporary culture's confusion about "church" was on prominent display.

Bloomburg's BusinessWeek website asked in a headline: "Can Crystal Cathedral Survive without its church?"[3] A distraught congregant mourned

1. Lathrop, *Holy People,* 9.

2. Cruz, Vives, and Landsberg, "O.C. Catholic diocese." Interestingly, the *congregation* of the Crystal Cathedral church disagreed with its leadership. It did *not* support the Diocesan bid. It is unclear if this was an expression of anti-Catholicism or hope that the University agreement would allow them to stay in the building for a longer period of time.

3. Taxin, "Can Crystal Cathedral survive?"

what he considered "the death of the church."[4] Another protested in a letter to the editor of the *OC Register*: "with all due respect, there is only one Christ, and He created only one, true Church; two thousand years ago, still extant today: the Holy Catholic Church, which purchased the cathedral."[5] In a telling comment, one congregant complained: "The cathedral's administration . . . have really stripped us of our ministry." Meanwhile, Shelia Schuller Coleman, the congregation's executive pastor, seeking to clarify, said, "Crystal Cathedral church is not a building. A church is comprised of people who are dedicated to practicing through words and works."[6] In this collection of quotations, it is easy to see the common equivalences assumed among building, congregation, broader assemblies, and even the work of Christ in which the church participates and to which it points. William Dyrness, a professor at nearby Fuller Theological Seminary, noted that the sale of the building was such a challenge because the *identity* of the congregation at the Crystal Cathedral is closely tied to its building.[7] Its core ministry—that is to say, its vocation—is understood to be its worship life (or perhaps, one might argue, in the missional television broadcast of its worship life), and that worship life is tied to, if not dependent upon, a particular building.

Indeed, worship is at the center of the church's vocation. From that center, the church goes into the world to do works of healing, service, and mission. It is also at the center of the church's identity. The church is "called out" from the world to know itself in worship. However, when the Diocese of Orange County begins its worshipping life in this same building, some of the core identifying elements of what was understood to be "church" will be gone: no more TV cameras, stage-lighting, and jumbotron screens. These will be replaced with a prominent pulpit, a baptismal font, and a high altar—not to mention a tabernacle, crucifix, and a *cathedra*. There will be scripture reading, prayer, and sacred song, but likely no celebrity guests, or

4. Bharath, "Crystal Cathedral board." Given the comments about the church's "death," it is interesting to note that the likely place where the Crystal Cathedral congregation will end up worshipping in 2014 is the St. Callistus Catholic Church building—named after the patron saint of graveyard caretakers.

5. "Letters," *Orange County Register*, November 21, 2011.

6. Taxin, "Crystal Cathedral sees risky future." Curiously, Coleman does not articulate precisely *what* words and works people are dedicated to practicing. But we can assume she is speaking of the imitation of Christ in word and deed that is part of Christian discipleship.

7. Taxin, "Crystal Cathedral sees risky future."

live "angels" suspended from the ceiling. The glass panes and steel scaffolding will remain, but the worship itself will be quite different, the congregation different, its leaders different, its links to other Christian communities different, and its understanding of its mission dramatically altered. Where is "church" in all this? In such a confused situation, how might anyone offer to this congregation, or to its community, pastoral consolation, pastoral rebuke, pastoral wisdom?

The ministry Robert A. Schuller birthed at the Crystal Cathedral is ecclesially liminal. The ministry is a part of the Reformed Church in America, the oldest Protestant denomination in the USA. It belongs to a broader RCA assembly—the California Classis—and its founding pastor was educated at one of the denomination's seminaries. But it is an outlier in many ways: its sunny Californian embrace of the "power of positive thinking," for example, is rather anomalous among its ecclesial kinfolk, dour Dutch Calvinists from the bustling east or the cloudy Midwest, comfortable—dare one say content—with the doctrine of total depravity. And its present leadership, in personnel and structure (commissioned pastors rather than ordained ministers guided by a self-selecting board of directors rather than an elected board of elders), raises eyebrows, if not disciplinary overtures, in many RCA circles. With its beginnings as a drive-in "community church" reaching out with a "message of encouragement and hope," its story is very familiar to the larger evangelical world of North American Protestantism, eager for the sake of the Gospel to appeal to popular culture through embrace and imitation of it. In this respect, it is, in many ways, a bellwether congregation—experiencing on a larger scale and a more public stage the same confusion about church and about worship that many Christian communities suffer.

METHODOLOGY

Ecclesiology. The theological discipline of ecclesiology—the study of "church"—is one of the places one turns to in order to sort these issues out. It has been a subject of considerable interest in the past century, owing perhaps to the increasing diversity in shapes and types of ministries, buildings, congregations, denominations, and other Christian-community affiliations.[8] Or maybe the diversity has been there all along, and in a world shrinking through easy travel and mass media, we are only now

---

8. See van Gelder, *Essence of the Church*, 15–20; and Gibbs, *ChurchNext*.

becoming more aware of it.[9] In any case, the proliferation of 'church' has been matched by a proliferation of ecclesiologies and ecclesiologists. Short patristic treatments of the topic, such as those by Irenaeus and Cyril, as well as Reformation-era treatments by Calvin and Melanchthon, are now joined by major works by contemporary Catholic, Orthodox, Reformed, Lutheran, Anglican, and Baptist theologians—among others. Even among free-church evangelicals, who are more well known for para-churches, mega-churches and all sorts of other prefixed people of God, there are pastors and theologians addressing this important topic.[10] Alongside these voices are theologians with ecumenical hearts, who explore the language and images used in Scripture for the church. They also articulate synthesis models for understanding the mystery of the church.[11]

Liturgical Theology. Alongside this renewed interest in ecclesiology and driven by the same ecumenical winds, there has now emerged another theological sub-discipline, liturgical theology.[12] The ecclesiological recovery in the early twentieth century of the model of the church as the mystical body of Christ was a key influence in the emergence of the liturgical renewal movement, and the coinciding development of the academic discipline of liturgical theology.[13] Work in this field focuses on one aspect of the church's life: its public worship and the relationship of that worship to what the church professes to believe. A shorthand for this dynamic is sometimes articulated in Latin terms as the relationship between the church's *lex orandi* and its *lex credendi*—its prayer and its belief. Questions of priority and normativity emerge here: which comes first, practices of prayer or instructions about how and what to pray? Likewise, questions

9. Veli-Matti Kärkkäinen suggests that the interest in ecclesiology is due to three factors: the emergence of the ecumenical movement, the growth of Christianity outside the west, and the rise of free-church congregations and communities across the globe. See Kärkkäinen, *Introduction to Ecclesiology*, 7–8.

10. Note that even a mass-market theologian like Rick Warren, Rev. Schuller's Southern California compatriot, has expanded his franchise in an ecclesiological direction. See Warren, *Purpose Driven Church*.

11. Dulles, *Models*, 2–3.

12. Interestingly, the relationship of liturgical theology and liturgiology—the much narrower study of liturgical rubrics—parallels the way the discipline of ecclesiology relates to the study of church buildings. See Irwin, "Liturgical Theology," 721–33; Schmemann, *Introduction to Liturgical Theology*, 9–13; and White, *Cambridge Movement*, 48–49.

13. See Pecklers, *Unread Vision*, especially 29–34. Cf. also Johnson, "State of Liturgical Renewal," 1–3.

of congruence are central to this discipline, as theologians ask whether a church's Eucharistic practices, for example, actually embody and reflect its doctrinal convictions about what happens at the table. There are varying approaches to these questions, but the fundamental task of liturgical theology is to reflect on worship and ask not only *what* do our liturgical actions mean but also *how* do they mean, and how we can understand worship as "the church's faith in motion."[14]

Liturgical Ecclesiology. At the intersection of these two disciplines is a relatively unplowed field in which there are a handful of committed teachers of the church exploring what is coming to be known as liturgical ecclesiology. In contrast to those who look first at scriptural, denominational, or sociological sources, "liturgical ecclesiologists" want to know what Christian *worship* can tell us about the church.[15] If indeed worship is at the heart of the church, then a theological exploration of worship and its normative sources should provide both insight and pastoral guidance for contemporary Christian communities, flailing about in accidental liturgical reform, seeking to articulate and live out some sense of what it means to be the people of God in a post-Christendom culture.

Though some scholars in this field do their work more self-consciously than others, there are a broad range of denominational traditions represented among those who are trying to look at church through liturgical spectacles. The most well-known such theologian, perhaps, is Gordon Lathrop, whose 2003 book, *Holy People* (a follow-up to his fundamental work in liturgical theology, *Holy Things*), quite explicitly gives the name "liturgical ecclesiology" to his "new attempt to say what Christian worship says of the church."[16] But others have come before and after, including: Geoffrey Wainwright, from the British Methodist tradition, whose *Doxology*—a systematic theology written from a liturgical perspective—has a significant section on ecclesiology and the marks of the church; Alexander Schmemann, the Orthodox scholar, who some consider the father of modern liturgical theology, whose writings on worship always have the church in view;[17] Simon Chan, an Assemblies of God/Pentecostal professor, whose

14. Kavanagh, *On Liturgical Theology*, 10. See also the fine introductory chapter on the grammar of liturgy in Fagerberg, *Theologia Prima*, 2–38.

15. Of course, Christian worship has scriptural, denominational, sociological, and other sources in its own right.

16. Lathrop, *Holy People*, 9.

17. See, for instance, this representative comment: "[Worship] is inseparable from the Church and without it there is no Church. But this is because its purpose is to express,

starting point for his liturgical theology is the "Church as a Worshipping Community;"[18] and the Roman Catholic priest Matthijs Ploeger, whose recent dissertation on comparative ecclesiologies looks explicitly at the doctrine of the church "from the angle of the liturgy."[19]

Almost all of these voices echo or appreciatively cite a single, influential, and yet often-overlooked theologian from the previous generation: Jean-Jacques von Allmen.[20] In this volume, it is my hope to begin to rectify this oversight by articulating a prototypical liturgical ecclesiology discerned in the writing of von Allmen and applying his insights to selected issues in the contemporary church.

JEAN-JACQUES VON ALLMEN

This book will explore the importance of Jean-Jacques von Allmen from four angles: historical, methodological, theological, and practical.

Historical. In the liturgical renewal movement of the twentieth century, von Allmen is often seen as the key figure from the Reformed tradition. He was a parish pastor in the Swiss village of Lucerne for seventeen years, and then professor of practical theology at the University of Neuchâtel from 1958 until his retiring in 1980 and his death in 1994. His theological work was always grounded in his experience of the local congregation at church and *as* church—a point to which we shall return repeatedly. A friend of Karl Barth, he worked tirelessly within his own confessional circle for liturgical reform. Yet he was broadly ecumenical in his sensibilities and appreciations. He helped found the Tantur Institute in Jerusalem, the scholarly journal *Studia Liturgica,* and he was one of the primary authors drafting the World Council of Church's key ecumenical achievement, the *Baptism, Eucharist, and Ministry* document. Perhaps he is best known for influential volumes on biblical theology (*A Companion to the Bible*), liturgical theology (*Worship: Its Theory and Practice, The Lord's Supper, Pastorale du Baptême, Prophétisme Sacramentel*) and homiletics (*Preaching & Congregation*). Though these works are widely admired and cited, they have

---

form, or realize the Church—to be the source of that grace which always makes the Church the Church" (Schmemann, *Introduction to Liturgical Theology*, 29).

18. Chan, *Liturgical Theology.*

19. Matthijs Ploeger, *Celebrating Church,* 3.

20. Lathrop, in particular, tips his hat to von Allmen in his methodological introduction to *Holy People.*

yet to be engaged or studied in any depth by subsequent generations of liturgical theologians.[21]

Methodological. Jean-Jacques von Allmen would not have recognized himself as a liturgical theologian (the term was not yet in use). He certainly would not have considered himself a pioneer in a theological sub-specialty named "Liturgical Ecclesiology."[22] Yet his work in both subject matter and methodological approach points clearly in this direction. For instance, a key passage in his primary volume on worship makes the following assertion—at once liturgical and ecclesiological:

> The study of dogmatic texts, of confessions of faith, of ecclesiastical disciplines, of the history of Christianity, of personal piety, important and essential as this is if one is to know the Church, is something that comes later: it is in the sphere of worship, the sphere par excellence where the life of the Church comes into being, that the fact of the Church first emerges. It is there that it gives proof of itself, there where it is focused, and where we are led when we truly seek it, and it is from that point that it goes out into the world to exercise its mission.[23]

21. For instance, Dwight Vogel's *Primary Sources of Liturgical Theology* excerpts a chapter of von Allmen's *Worship*, and Arlo Duba (writing in an introduction) identifies von Allmen as the "premier liturgical theologian in and for the Reformed tradition" (Vogel, *Primary Sources,* 127). Likewise, Tom Long writes that von Allmen's *Preaching and Congregation* is "a high-water mark in Reformed homiletics" (Long, "Distance We Have Traveled," 11). Ron Byars's volume in the *Interpretation* series on *Sacraments in Biblical Perspective* opens with von Allmen's articulation of the challenge the sacraments pose to churches "influenced by long exposure to the Enlightenment" (Byars, *Sacraments,* 1). Apart from frequent comments like these, about a dozen articles deal directly with J.-J. von Allmen. There are no major works on von Allmen's liturgical theology, though a festschrift was published in his honor (see Congar, *Communio Sanctorum*). In addition, a number of studies have set von Allmen's thought alongside other theologians' as a point of comparison. Nicholas Wolterstorff, for example, chooses von Allmen and Schmemann as his two primary interlocutors in his book of liturgical theology (Wolterstorff, *God We Worship*). See also Old, *Holy Communion,* 835–56. A handful of dissertations also deal with von Allmen, including: Agnew, *Concept of Sacrifice;* Cuminetti, *Element "cattolici";* Barot and Prosperi, *Il movimento ecumenico;* Townsend, *Sacramentality of Preaching;* and Ploeger, *Celebrating Church.*

22. He considered himself as working within the field of "practical theology"—a field which has undergone significant transformation in the past decades. For more on these developments, see Anderson, *Shape of Practical Theology;* and Maddox, "Practical Theology," 159–69.

23. von Allmen, *Worship,* 43–44.

If one wishes to learn about the church, argues von Allmen, one must look first to the church *at* church. That is to say, if one wishes to do ecclesiology, the starting point is the worshipping congregation by God's grace undertaking the work of the people: gathering to hear the Word preached, to celebrate the Lord's Supper, to initiate by water new members into the life of the Holy Spirit, and to be sent into the world. The church at worship is the manifestation—the epiphany, the revelation—of the church.

Theological. This theological assertion is one of three central themes that appear in nearly all of von Allmen's writings. Alongside them is his understanding of the church's worship as the recapitulation of the history of salvation. And third, his sense that the church in relation to the world is both promise and threat.[24] These are generative ideas that can lead the curious inquirer in many directions: What is the mechanism by which the church comes to know itself at worship? What is the relationship of the church to Christ and the salvation that comes through him? How does the church's mission find expression within its worship life? What does the church's present life have to do with God's past and God's future? What are the liturgical signs of the church's most fundamental ecclesiological characteristics: its unity, holiness, catholicity, and apostolicity?

Practical. These are precisely the sorts of ecclesiological questions that one might profitably ask von Allmen. And the answers that emerge will have particular resonance in today's world, as many of the impinging crises of von Allmen's day have only grown more acute in the intervening years: the challenge of ecumenism and a church that professes unity, yet seems ever more divided; the church's diverse and rapidly changing worship practices, a sense that many of these practices are profoundly detrimental to Christian formation, and a helplessness in seeking normative standards of theological and liturgical excellence; an ecclesiological shallowness in the evangelical church, confessed and highlighted in, for instance, the "Chicago Call" in 1977.[25]

Furthermore, a liturgical ecclesiology derived from von Allmen may have the capability to speak directly to practical ministry problems that appear where the evangelical and the reformed streams flow together in

24. These are not entirely original theological themes—Ireneus takes a rather convincing turn on recapitulation, for instance—but von Allmen makes these three central to all of his writings about worship, sacraments, preaching, and church. See Bürki, "Jean-Jacques von Allmen dans le Mouvement Liturgique," 52–61.

25. See Webber, *Common Roots,* Appendix I. See also "Chicago Call," and Chan, *Liturgical Theology,* 9–17.

the riverbed of North American Protestantism—problems like those that plagued the Crystal Cathedral about the church's identity. And perhaps more significantly, they may speak helpfully into conversations surrounding a wider cluster of problems that we will address in the last section of this book—such as questions about infant vs. believer baptism, the gifts and graces of the Holy Spirit, and the meaning of church membership; questions about who may fruitfully be invited to and receive God's grace at the Eucharist; questions about the structure of worship and the salvation story it invites people to witness to in worship; questions about worship space and its capacity to open congregations to God's transformative activity; questions about the church's missional vocation in and to the world; and questions in homiletics about the turn to the listener, embodied proclamation, and the relationship between word, table, and font. Jean-Jacques von Allmen's confessional location and ecumenical experience makes him perhaps uniquely suited to bridge present gaps between mainline liturgical traditions and word-centered evangelical traditions.

We will see that the liturgical ecclesiology that emerges from von Allmen's thought exhibits Reformed sensibilities, has deep roots in both Scripture and the broader Christian tradition, reflects rich ecumenical conversations as well as day-to-day work in and commitment to local congregations, and provides fuel for important practical thinking about the church's place and work in the world.

Summary. The purpose of this book, then, is to do what we have been describing: to examine the sacramental, homiletical, and liturgical writings of Jean-Jacques von Allmen in order to discern and reconstruct a "liturgical ecclesiology" there—i.e., an articulation of the way in which the church's worship, sacraments, and preaching shape the church's identity. I will argue that von Allmen was a pioneering theologian working this new field, doing liturgical theology *as* ecclesiology. To do so, I will employ a classic ecclesiological lens—the Nicene marks—and look through it to gain focus in my study of von Allmen's writings on worship, preaching, and the sacraments. This theological analysis will then provide us with tools for practical and pastoral thinking about the church's place and work in the world today. The tools will also help us to discern where von Allmen's contributions to conversations in liturgical theology and in ecclesiology are especially helpful, and where they may need further development or correction by the next generation of scholars.

The Path Ahead. A first chapter on method will locate the present study within the academic conversations and respective disciplines of ecclesiology and liturgical theology. It will offer a definition of "liturgical ecclesiology" and characterize von Allmen as a prototypical theologian working this new field. This technical chapter will be more interesting and meaningful for scholars in the field; others may wish to begin with the second chapter, a brief biographical sketch of von Allmen's life and work. This biographical chapter will contextualize the constructive theology which follows. The third and fourth chapters will first examine von Allmen's liturgical theology through the three key themes previously mentioned, and then through the Nicene lens of the church's identifying characteristics: one, holy, catholic, and apostolic. The fifth chapter turns to what Lathrop would call "pastoral" liturgical ecclesiology—theology with an eye on *reforming* practices through both description and prescription, seeking congruence between the church's *credendi* and *orandi*. A brief section on liturgical and homiletical implications will then apply the results of this interchange to some contemporary problems.

CHAPTER 1

Liturgical Ecclesiology

The Church is first and foremost a worshipping community. Worship comes first, doctrine and discipline second.

—GEORGE FLOROVSKY[1]

WHAT IS LITURGICAL ECCLESIOLOGY? A part of what this present project aims to do is to identify an emerging field at the intersection of two fairly new theological disciplines: ecclesiology and liturgical theology. It will first be necessary to provide some context—thematic, historical, and methodological—in order to locate the present project within those larger disciplinary conversations.

PIONEERS AND SUBSEQUENT SETTLERS

On the border between ecclesiology and liturgical theology is a relatively undeveloped theological subdivision. In what follows, my intention is to take some of the *materials* from the one neighborhood (liturgical theology) along with the best *plans* from what we might consider to be well-constructed houses in the neighborhood of ecclesiology, to see what kind of structure von Allmen, as a pioneer, built there. Or to use another metaphor, I want to put on a pair of ecclesiological spectacles—in particular (though

1. Florovsky, "Elements of Liturgy," 2.

1

not exclusively), the Nicene marks of the church—and read von Allmen's liturgical theology through them. What we see there will be a new thing: a liturgical ecclesiology.[2] We will begin with a brief examination of a few theologians who, consciously or not, followed in von Allmen's footsteps, whose work and methodologies echo those von Allmen used decades earlier, and who, self-consciously or not, were also doing liturgical ecclesiology. Our goal is to be particularly attentive to their methodological moves. We will then be in a position to articulate the approach that will guide the rest of this study.

The connection between liturgy and ecclesiology is an obvious one, but not a clear one. That is to say, while it is plain to see that there is a connection, it is more difficult to define precisely what that connection is. Recent interest in both fields of study has led a few scholars—especially liturgical theologians—to try to do so. For example, as the Orthodox theologian Alexander Schmemann writes in his *Introduction to Liturgical Theology*: "The purpose of worship is to constitute the Church."[3] Hence, his methodological approach is to start with the church at worship, its liturgical life, and its fundamental *ordo*, and to discern in them the material for theological—and thus ecclesiological—reflection. In contrast, Lutheran scholar Frank Senn suggests a mirror image of this relationship between the two: liturgy and the study of it is encompassed by ecclesiological questions and concerns. He writes that liturgiology (a cousin of liturgical theology) is really "a subdivision of ecclesiology."[4]

The recovery of the doctrine of the Mystical Body of Christ was central to the emergence of the Liturgical Renewal Movement, and to liturgical theology as its own discipline. The fundamental conviction arising from this recovery is that the church is most explicitly itself when it gathers on the Lord's Day for worship. This is the starting point and returning touchstone for nearly all of the scholars who, like von Allmen, undertake to do

---

2. This way of combining theological sub-disciplines (Liturgical Theology + *something else*) is not entirely novel. Don Saliers's important work, *Divine Glory*, for example, is a model of what one might call liturgical *eschatology*: "This book stands at the intersection of three pathways of reflection: liturgical studies, theological aesthetics, and eschatology" (Saliers, *Worship as Theology*, 13). Consider another example, Clay Schmit's recent *Sent and Gathered*, which is an attempt to take the "missional" impulse in ecclesiology seriously, and to outline what its liturgical implications might be.

3. Schmemann, *Introduction*, 19.

4. "The story of liturgy is inseparable from the community that performs liturgical orders as its public work" (Senn, *Christian Liturgy*, xv).

liturgical theology from an ecclesiological viewpoint. Hearing, in the pages that follow, from later settlers in this territory (or, to use the other metaphor, those who wore ecclesiological glasses while writing their liturgical theology) will give us some guidelines to discern the method and assess the prototypical liturgical ecclesiology we see in von Allmen.

Nathan Mitchell

In 1999, Nathan Mitchell published an article entitled *Liturgy and Ecclesiology*. His is an interpretation of Vatican II as a reform of both worship and church—or perhaps, church *through* worship: "The challenge of Vatican II, therefore, was not simply to find a new way of worshipping, but to find a new way of being church in and for the world."[5] For Mitchell, as for Schmemann and Kavanagh, doctrine arises from doxology—ecclesiology from liturgy:

> Patterned on Christ, led by the Spirit, embodied in the Gospels, and enacted in the liturgy. . . . Through them the Christian assembly rehearses—practices—the presence of God's kingdom in and for the world. For this reason, liturgy is the privileged place where the Church discovers and actualizes its own deepest identity.[6]

Mitchell hastens to note that liturgy is not just a set of institutional rituals or body of beliefs, but a way of life.

For Mitchell, the presence of God's kingdom is characterized by radical renunciation of money, glory, and power. It is a community in which economic, racial, and sexual barriers have fallen. It is a community where people own things in common, willingly and quickly offer forgiveness, where they shoulder each other's burdens, etc.[7] "This," says Mitchell, "is the ecclesiology that the liturgy rehearses and promotes." Then, he places that ecclesiology in God's salvation history: "It offers not only an ideal icon of who and what the Church should be but a lively sacrament of the whole world's future."[8] Ecclesiology, eschatology, and ethics all intersect,

---

5. Mitchell, "Liturgy and Ecclesiology," 118.

6. Mitchell, "Liturgy and Ecclesiology," 119.

7. Mitchell's picture of this community is borrowed from a beautiful passage by Mateos, "Message of Jesus," 12.

8. Mitchell, "Liturgy and Ecclesiology," 122.

as the church calls itself and the world into a destiny of justice, peace, and charity—a destiny that must simultaneously be sought after and rested in.

The method for a liturgical ecclesiology that Mitchell outlines, then, is one characterized "not only by an emphasis on the Church's cultic activity but also—and more importantly—by its emphasis on the Church as a body of disciples who enflesh Jesus' vision of a new human community based on justice, mercy, and compassion."[9] In other words, the worshipping church is important, but important *because* it is there that the Christian community's values for life in the world are shaped and expressed. It is there that the body of Christ is formed. Mitchell identifies two specific consequences. First, that Eucharistic hospitality is the hallmark of any community that is called church. This puts the Lord's Supper at the center not only of liturgical celebrations, but also of Christian life. Second, there is a humility vis-à-vis the world, an acknowledgment of a "liturgy in the world," a grace that God gives the cosmos at its depths, which is signaled but not exhausted in the Eucharist. Thus, the supper is not an invitation to abandonment of the "secular," but an offering the church makes, an offering of Christ, and itself, as sacrament for the world.

Mitchell's article, while suggestive, has neither the length nor the focus to clearly articulate either a method for liturgical ecclesiology or a constructive project of liturgical ecclesiology. But it is significant in its use of the term and the centrality of ecclesiological issues addressed through worship.

Geoffrey Wainwright

Twenty years earlier, in 1980, the British Methodist Geoffrey Wainwright published his landmark work of liturgical theology, *Doxology: The Praise of God in Worship, Doctrine, and Life*. The work is comprehensive; his goal is to produce an entire systematic theology "from a liturgical perspective."[10] Thus, a significant portion of the first part of this work is devoted to ecclesiology. The methodology he employs in this section is consonant with von Allmen's own—looking primarily at the four Nicene Marks. The connections are clear, as Wainwright developed a von Allmen-esque liturgical ecclesiology.[11]

9. Mitchell, "Liturgy and Ecclesiology," 123.

10. Wainwright, *Doxology*, ix.

11. It is interesting to note some of Wainwright's connections with Jean-Jacques von

Wainwright begins this section by locating the church's worshiping life within God's salvation history.[12] He first notes the tension that exists between definitions and descriptions of the church that emerge from scripture and the creeds, and the reality of our experience of church. His primary distinction, then, is not between a "visible" and an "invisible" church, but rather between the "eschatological" and the "actual."[13] The tension the church experiences is between itself in the present, and the future self it is called into becoming. Yet this tension is also created, in part, by the past, by the recollection of God's action in history. The actions are not merely remembered, but these "primal events" are inserted into human time, creating the expectation of a "new deliverance," patterned after the previous ones. This dynamic is seen most clearly in the sacraments, which "express ritually the fact that the historical Church is definitely on the way to that perfect glorification and enjoyment of God which is God's purpose for humanity."[14]

Wainwright then turns to the Nicene marks of the church, citing von Allmen in support of his contention that the church realizes its most fundamental identity when it is worshiping: "Taking up the thought of J.-J. von Allmen that the true face of Church's self-description in the Nicene Creed come to expression in liturgical practice."[15]

At the outset of his discussion, Wainwright marshals the biblical evidence for the church's calling to unity. His attention turns quickly to baptism, to the allegedly "one" baptism the un-unified church celebrates, and to the ecumenical problems of mutual recognition of other churches. He draws a direct connection between the 'unrepeatability' of Christ's death and the unrepeatability of baptism through which the baptized participates in Christ's death and resurrection. Likewise, if baptism is not to devolve into magic, it must involve some degree of intentionality on the part of the minister and recipient (or a recipient's representative).

Allmen, including his translation into English of some of von Allmen's best articles, their joint service to the Faith & Order Commission of the WCC during the 1980s, and Wainwright's service as president of the *Societas Liturgica* after von Allmen's retirement. Significantly, in a hefty footnote citing dozens of liturgical theologies, von Allmen gets first reference. See Wainwright, *Doxology*, 464.

12. Mitchell also began here, and as we will see, so does von Allmen.

13. Wainwright, *Doxology*, 118.

14. Wainwright, *Doxology*, 121.

15. Wainwright, *Doxology*, 122.

Wainwright turns next to the church's holiness. He focuses on three central biblical *images* for the church: the people of God, the body of Christ, and those indwelt by the Holy Spirit. Again, he turns first to baptism as the signal practice of a holy people who have been washed clean by a gracious God. Connecting doctrine, worship, and *life*, Wainwright then turns to the importance of the ethical implications of baptism, and the need for the church and its members to die persistently that they might rise. He mentions, unusually, Communion as an "occasion for the affirmation of God's judgment upon sin" and thus the invitation to or preparation for Communion as an opportunity to rehearse repentance and forgiveness. He concludes by underscoring the importance of regular confession and absolution as a way of ritually managing the eschatological tension of a people called to be holy, made holy by baptism, and yet, even after baptism, persisting in sin.[16]

The catholicity of the church, according to Wainwright, is grounded in the universality of its Savior, the universality of the salvation intended for "all nations," the universality of the Holy Spirit being poured out "on all flesh," and most significantly, the universality connected throughout scripture with the Messianic banquet, the Eucharist, and its precedents. Jesus offers his own blood as the sign of the new covenant, poured out for "many."[17] The sovereignty of Christ becomes the rationale for Wainwright's observations concerning the exclusion of women from office as "untrue to the church's vocation to catholicity."[18] He concludes with a practical and personal example of the sort of catholicity that can find expression in a world of global connection: the English-speaking church he served in French Cameroon, in which people from many denominational backgrounds and geographic homes were able to worship together and offer their gifts to the community in submission to the Lordship of Christ.

Wainwright's take on the church's apostolicity is rather straightforward: he speaks of God's mission in and to the world—a mission now embodied in a message and in messengers. The message itself is found first in the Gospel, then in the scriptures (as they witness to the Good News in Jesus Christ), and then, via the church's interpretation, in the ecumenical

16. Wainwright, *Doxology*, 127–32.

17. Wainwright, *Doxology*, 133. Wainwright appreciatively cites Jeremias's argument that the synoptic phrase in the institution narrative has an inclusive meaning: not "many, but not all" but "all, who are many."

18. Wainwright, *Doxology*, 134.

creeds. He recognizes the classic division between East and West, locating the continuity of apostolic succession in either message or messenger. And he concludes with a quick look at ordination services whose practices (including laying on of hands, etc.) signify the identification of church leaders, the recognition of the same by the laity, and the community's dependence upon God.

To conclude his section on the church, Wainwright takes up the three Pauline virtues—faith, hope, and love—to see how they might inform an exploration of the composition of the church from a liturgical perspective. Beginning with "faith," Wainwright addresses the question of infant baptism and finds only one theological understanding that properly relates God's grace to human faith. His stand—much like von Allmen's—is to avoid infant baptism in order to preserve the freedom that is at the heart of the kingdom vision into which any Christian is baptized.[19] Addressing the virtue Love, relative to church composition, Wainwright notes that the liturgy makes plain that members of the church are integrated into a body, a community of believers. In this body, individuality is respected, while the sacraments especially are celebrated by those who come together. Other liturgical expressions of this communal love are seen in the kiss of peace and in singing, where the congregation experiences the unifying force of rhythm and melody.[20] Wainwright points to Eucharist and preaching as places where the individuality of the presider and the commonality of the assembly are both necessary. Finally, the question of how the church relates to those of other faiths is taken up in Wainwright's section on hope, where he rejects both the stern exclusivism of Tertullian and a wide-open but Constantinian inclusivism that can "strike even well-disposed adherents of other faiths as Christian imperialism by dint of unwanted annexation."[21] As so frequently before, the liturgical point of view is taken by standing next to the baptismal font, where Wainwright sees baptism as a non-exclusive and hopeful promise: here, at least, in the baptismal waters, God is at work saving people.[22]

---

19. Wainwright, *Doxology*, 139–41.

20. Wainwright, *Doxology*, 143.

21. Wainwright, *Doxology*, 144.

22. The hope is found in the non-exclusive character of the promise. God may be at work in many places, evidenced by the patterns of salvation: "dying to sin and self; living for God and for fellow human beings; filial growth into the moral likeness of the Creator; openness to the transforming Spirit" (Wainwright, *Doxology*, 145).

A few summary observations concerning the method of this liturgical ecclesiology: First, Wainwright begins each section in the ecclesiological chapter of *Doxology* with a survey of the scripture that informs his discussion. This demonstrates that his starting point is *not* worship. That is to say, it is not what liturgical theologians like Aidan Kavanagh might call *theologia prima* nor the liturgical assembly itself, but scripture.[23] His intention is clearly to ground his theology in the Bible. It is less clear whether he intends to use scripture as his primary source to norm present practice. When he speaks with methodological clarity about the entire project, he puts it this way: "There is properly a complementary and harmonious relationship between worship and doctrine, and that it is the business of worship and doctrine to express the Christian truth."[24] At the same time, he speaks in the introduction about the precedence of the Christian "vision" transmitted to him by the Christian community. That vision guides the community's life in the world, but it finds sharp focus and "concentrated expression" in worship. The theologian's task is to express coherently that vision in doctrine. Doing so, the theologian looks at worship both to learn from it and to offer correction or improvement to it.[25]

Second, it is significant to note that Wainwright makes the Nicene marks the centerpiece of his proto-liturgical ecclesiology. Yet even as he does so, he offers no explicit rationale for this choice, no argument for why these descriptive adjectives are a better way into an ecclesiological discussion than any others. This is no fault; ecclesiologists of nearly every stripe have found it both helpful and even necessary to explore the identity of the church through these foundational and scriptural descriptors: one, holy, catholic, and apostolic. It is, indeed, the method in this book as well.

Finally, we note that Wainwright does not have any corresponding section concerning the church's *activity* to go along with his discussion of the church's *identity*. His focus is more abstractly theological, thus he gives little attention to what the church *does*. When he does speak of activities, he focuses primarily on the sacraments, and his treatment of these is mostly theoretical rather than practical. He offers only incidental discussion of the assembly's liturgical activities other than preaching, the Lord's Supper, and baptism. And he offers hardly any discussion at all—in this ecclesiological

23. Kavanagh, *On Liturgical Theology*, 134, cited in Johnson, "Liturgy and Theology," 225.

24. Wainwright, *Doxology*, 252.

25. Wainwright, *Doxology*, 3.

section—on the ways the church enacts and expresses the kingdom vision by which the Holy Spirit animates the community in its everyday life, as well as the distillation of this vision expressed in its worship on the Lord's Day.[26] For example, his discussion of the church's unity focuses almost exclusively on baptism, not on any other liturgical moment such as the prayers of the people. It is not as if these things are seen as unimportant—he does speak of the unifying force of rhythm and melody in the section on love—but they are clearly secondary to Wainright's project.

We now turn to another scholar from a very different denominational tradition, whose recent work of liturgical theology is so thoroughly focused on the church that it, too, might be understood to be a kind of unnamed liturgical ecclesiology.

Simon Chan

Though he received his PhD from Cambridge, Simon Chan comes from a very different starting point than Geoffrey Wainwright. A self-identified evangelical from the Pentecostal Assemblies of God, Chan lives and works in Singapore, representing a new generation of theologians from a new part of the world and a new quarter of the church. Like Wainwright, he writes with deep appreciation for the long-standing liturgical tradition of the church. His book, *Liturgical Theology: The Church as Worshipping Community*, is not a comprehensive systematic theology. It is (rather obviously) a work of liturgical theology. Yet, like the pioneer von Allmen, the questions he seems centrally concerned with are deeply *ecclesiological* questions. Thus, his work resonates in substance and method with what von Allmen and others are doing: liturgical ecclesiology.

The thrust of the argument Chan makes in this book is this: "The problem of ecclesiology plaguing modern evangelicalism cannot be

26. Which is not to say that these concerns are not at all in Wainwright's view. In fact, in a more comprehensive examination of Wainwright's thought, we might also look at his more recent *Worship with One Accord*. It, too, might be considered another sort of "proto" liturgical ecclesiology, focusing quite specifically on questions surrounding the church's relationship with other churches. In that book, Wainwright explores the connections between the Ecumenical Movement and the Liturgical Movement. In the introduction, he writes: "Worship is intimately connected with doctrine, discipline, social organization, ethical conduct, charitable action, testimony to Christ" (Wainwright, *Worship*, vii). Significantly, the opening and closing citations in Wainwright's chapter on "The Church as a Worshipping Community" comes from von Allmen, demonstrating his debt to the Swiss theologian's pioneering work.

separated from the problem of worship."[27] Evangelicals have an unhealthy church largely because of flawed theology. Specifically, they have a flawed, rationalistic, nearly gnostic ecclesiology. In this view, the church is primarily instrumental, using rationalistic means for the primary (and mostly anthropocentric) purpose of saving souls. Chan argues that this sense of what the church is and what the church does are intimately tied to a flawed understanding of worship. The solution he proposes is a renewal of ecclesiology through a renewal of worship—worship grounded in the historical liturgical practices of the Church.

The next section will not so much *summarize* the content of Chan's argument but rather see how its content and its contours—i.e., the questions he finds significant and the manner in which he presents those questions—reveal his methodological approach.

One of Jean-Jacques von Allmen's theological touchstones is that worship is the "manifestation" of the church. Chan begins his argument in the same place von Allmen does: with the assertion that worship is the fundamental defining activity of the church. "The church's most basic identity is to be found in its act of worship."[28] Worship, he declares, is what distinguishes church *as* church; there may be other things the church does—champion the poor, preserve social values, etc.—but these do not make it the church. In fact, von Allmen looms large as a figure throughout Chan's book. He is quoted often and at length, and many of his key ideas are referenced and articulated early in Chan's work, setting the stage for what is to follow. For example, early on, Chan speaks of the church standing over and against the world, as a "threat" to it.[29] He notes that worship *realizes* or constitutes the church as an ontological reality.[30] He locates the church and its worship within the narrative of God's salvation history, remembered and anticipated in the anamnesis and epiclesis of the Eucharistic celebration.[31] All these themes, as we will see, are central in von Allmen's liturgical ecclesiology.

When Chan explicitly takes up questions of methodology, he offers a nice summary of the *lex orandi/lex credendi* debate that has often animated methodological conversations in the field of liturgical theology.

27. Chan, *Liturgical Theology*, 41.

28. Chan, *Liturgical Theology*, 42.

29. Chan, *Liturgical Theology*, 42–43.

30. Chan, *Liturgical Theology*, 46.

31. Chan, *Liturgical Theology*, 36–37.

Chan affirms a reciprocal or dialectical relationship between *orandi* and *credendi*,[32] but he argues more strongly than one might expect from an evangelical scholar for the proper influence of the *orandi*, speaking from his experience of many evangelical congregations: "The primary theology expressed in a heterodox *ordo* will quickly overwhelm an isolated orthodox belief, making it totally irrelevant to the life of the church."[33] He argues that one of the problems in the evangelical church today is the inability to see worship itself as a *theologia prima*.[34]

Like Aidan Kavanagh and Alexander Schmemann, he argues that the *orandi* can and should shape the church's *credendi* as a historical, ecumenical, and normative liturgical *ordo*. In this, he follows Dix's *The Shape of the Liturgy*. He avoids contemporary critiques of Dix by holding on to an *ordo* that is surprisingly simple—far less specific than Dix's or Schmemann's, and less nuanced than Lathrop's "juxtaposition" approach.[35] For Chan, the *ordo* is really one thing: word and sacrament,[36] distinct, yet inseparable, and mutually reinforcing. In this way, too, he follows von Allmen (and many others) in critiquing those communities that have subordinated or neglected either one.[37] Worship—and by extension, the church—is fundamentally sacramental and specifically Eucharistic.

This adjective—Eucharistic—points us to another feature of Chan's liturgical ecclesiology: his treatment of the church's identity and consequent activity, a strong reformation theme. Chan clearly distinguishes identity from activity—though he does so, in some way, in order to conflate them again. For Chan, the fundamental *identity* of the church is seen in *the fundamental activity* of the church—worship. He begins by exploring the "ontology" of the church using three biblical images: the people of God, the

---

32. Chan, *Liturgical Theology*, 48–49.

33 Chan, *Liturgical Theology*, 52. In this section, he offers a sharp critique of the common frontier *ordo* of "singing-sermon-singing," in which worship is understood to be little more than time for instruction in the truth of the faith, and that truth understood as right belief, promulgated in the sermon, not embodied in the liturgical structure.

34 Chan, *Liturgical Theology*, 52.

35. See section on Lathrop below.

36. Chan, *Liturgical Theology*, 52.

37. Chan, *Liturgical Theology*, 65. In fact, Chan quotes von Allmen appreciatively in his critique of evangelical traditions in which the Supper is regarded as optional, or in which it is celebrated only occasionally. To do so, they both argue, is to undermine the church's claim to catholicity.

body of Christ, and the temple of the Holy Spirit.[38] When he speaks of the Church as the body of Christ, he says that this is not just a metaphor, but an 'ontological reality': the Church is Christ, embodied for the world in the time between the ascension and the parousia.[39] In this connection, he offers a robust and Roman Catholic-friendly defense of "tradition" as crucial to the church's sense of itself, the "means by which the church understands its true identity . . . in historical continuity with the church of the past."[40]

Chan also draws upon his own Pentecostal tradition to explore the work of the Spirit within the church. It is the Spirit who links the church to Christ and gives the people of God its distinctly eschatological character. The Holy Spirit is the epiphany of Christ in the church, both the gift of God and the giver of gifts.[41] He asserts:

> The one church is *one* precisely because it is united to Christ the Head by the one Spirit who indwells it, making it the one temple of the Spirit and the one body of Christ. The church is *holy* precisely because it is the temple indwelled by the Holy Spirit. The church is *apostolic* precisely because the Spirit guides it into all truth and preserves it from error by binding it diachronically to the apostles in an unbroken succession.[42]

One can hear echoes here of the Mystical Body of Christ theology: his exploration of the identifying Nicene marks of the church is offered in direct connection with his thinking about the relationship between pneumatology and ecclesiology.

The Nicene marks—one, holy, catholic, apostolic—are not the only adjectives Chan sees as helpful in defining the church's identity. When he speaks of the church's basic *ordo* as word and sacrament, bound together, he argues that both these liturgical movements are: a) rooted in the incarnation; b) Eucharistic in orientation; c) eschatological in horizon; d) missiological in purpose. That is to say, he spends significant energy expounding on four descriptive adjectives for worship that are supplemental to the

38. These are the same images that Lesslie Newbigin uses in his foundational ecclesiological treatment, *The Household of God*. But Chan's use of the images is quite different from Newbigin's.

39. Chan, *Liturgical Theology*, 28.

40. Chan, *Liturgical Theology*, 31.

41. Chan, *Liturgical Theology*, 34.

42. Chan, *Liturgical Theology*, 36. Interestingly, Chan does not address here the *catholicity* of the church in connection with the Holy Spirit—a connection that we will see von Allmen makes quite clearly.

Nicene marks: incarnational, Eucharistic, eschatological, and missiological.[43] Many of these terms are significant for von Allmen as well. And these same adjectives can be applied just as fruitfully to the church itself as well as its foundational activity, worship.

The postmodern preference for the concrete over the abstract has led, argues Chan, to a recent shift in ecclesiological emphasis from what the church *is* to what the church *does*—activity rather than identity. Such an approach deals with the church not merely as an 'ideal' institution but also takes into account its weaknesses and failures. It acknowledges that the church is not only about doctrine or description but also about a "distinctive way of life."[44] And so, Chan also explores some basic activities of the church, or *practices*.

He begins by acknowledging that the relationship between practice and ecclesial formation is "not as straightforward as commonly assumed."[45] It is hard to map good practices within the Christian community on to good practices in the world. Generosity in one realm, for example, does not necessarily follow from generosity in the other. Furthermore, it is hard, even in a given congregation, to assume common understanding and intentionality of good practices. (For Chan, understanding and intentionally are crucial to formation; it cannot happen without them.) Chan's solution is to see the church's liturgy (Word plus sacrament) as the "essential and primary practice" from which all the others flow:

> The deep structure underlying the church's liturgy conveys a primary theology that gives the practice of the liturgy its inner coherence and shapes the church into a coherent community. It is from this coherent liturgy that other secondary practices derive their significance as Christian practices.[46]

Thus, Chan distinguishes between the "essential" practices of the church—those that constitute the church as church—and others, like hospitality, that emerge from and are grounded in word and sacrament.[47] The second half of the book explores these "secondary" practices in more detail. Though there might be many, Chan focuses on three: the catechumenate, the four-fold *ordo* of the Sunday liturgy, and active participation in worship—or what he

43. Chan, *Liturgical Theology*, 36–40.
44. Chan, *Liturgical Theology*, 85.
45. Chan, *Liturgical Theology*, 86.
46. Chan, *Liturgical Theology*, 87.
47. Chan, *Liturgical Theology*, 88.

calls "liturgical spirituality," which links liturgy and life. In these sections, he deals more explicitly with other parts of the Lord's Day worship service. For example, he addresses the creed, the Decalogue, and the Lord's Prayer as places within the Lord's Day liturgy for the catechumenate to take hold—where ecclesial mystagogy can take place.[48] Likewise, he offers instruction to worship leaders and participants to aid in their "full, conscious, active participation," and has specific advice for those who deploy their musical gifts in the service of the church's worship.[49]

Summary. The liturgical theology articulated by Chan focuses primarily on what the church's worship says about what it is and does. In other words, his liturgical theology, like von Allmen's, is a *de facto* liturgical ecclesiology. It is especially in this last section that Chan turns to what Gordon Lathrop will call "pastoral" liturgical theology—where abstract musings about the church meet its concrete activities. We will make this same turn in the concluding section of the present study. But first, we offer a survey of the first theologian to explicitly identify his work as a product of "liturgical ecclesiology": Gordon Lathrop.

GORDON LATHROP

Holy Things: A Liturgical Theology, published in 1993, was the first of three books in liturgical theology written by Gordon Lathrop, a Lutheran scholar with deep ecumenical experience and commitments.[50] In an elegant and poetic style, the book articulated a methodology for doing theology through the eyes of liturgy. This methodology then guided him in two subsequent volumes as he explored a "liturgical cosmology" and a "liturgical ecclesiology."[51] Thus, in Lathrop we have the key paradigm for what we are doing in this book: grounding "an ecumenical vision of ecclesial life and theology in the central activities of worship."[52] We will summarize Lathrop's

48. In this, Chan closely echoes Robert Webber's *Ancient-Future Evangelism.*

49. Chan, *Liturgical Theology,* 156–58.

50. Lathrop was a participant in the Faith and Order consultations on worship and Christian unity through the 1990s,. Through an international study team of the Lutheran World Federation, he has been engaged in research on the links between liturgy and culture, liturgy and ethics, and liturgy and mission. He is also a member of *Societas Liturgica* and past president of the North American Academy of Liturgy.

51. See Lathrop, *Holy Things; Holy People;* and *Holy Ground.*

52. Saliers, "Review of *Holy People,*" 30.

methodological approach to both liturgical theology and, more specifically, liturgical ecclesiology.

Liturgical theology, for Lathrop, is about discerning the meaning of the church's worship life. It asks "how the Christian meeting, in all its signs and words, says something authentic and reliable about God, and so says something true about ourselves and our world as they are understood before God."[53] As he explains further, his methodology is characterized by three features: a distinction between primary, secondary, and tertiary or "pastoral" liturgical theology; a juxtaposition of dialectical elements, particularly strong symbols; and an identification of the "central things" of the church's worship (book, bath, and table).

Lathrop follows many liturgical theologians in distinguishing between "primary" and "secondary" liturgical theology. For Lathrop, primary liturgical theology is "the communal meaning of the liturgy exercised by the gathering itself."[54] In this, Lathrop follows Kavanagh and many others who identify as primary meaning-making what the church actually does when it assembles to worship the Triune God. Lathrop gives particular importance to the use of the church's primary *symbols* in its worship. Secondary liturgical theology is reflection on primary theology. It is "written and spoken discourse that attempts to find words for the experience of the liturgy and to illuminate its structures, intending to enable a more profound participation in those structures by members of the assembly."[55] Note the "reforming edge" present in this description. Lathrop writes explicitly that secondary liturgical theology is "not merely descriptive" but rather that it always has a kind of renewal in view—a renewal of understanding or, in some cases, a renewal of practice. When the renewing force of secondary liturgical theology is "turned to specific problems of our time," he calls these reflections pastoral liturgical theology.[56]

Also central to Lathrop's methodology is juxtaposition. The truth, he suggests, is spoken in two words, not just one. Theology is full of these sorts of dialectical pairs: God as immanent and transcendent, the already-but-not-yet of the eschaton, etc. In a similar way, the juxtaposition of two

53. Lathrop, *Holy Things*, 3.

54. Lathrop, *Holy Things*, 5.

55. Lathrop, *Holy Things*, 6. That Lathrop finds the ultimate *telos* of secondary theology in the "more profound participation" of congregants in the assembly's worship is testimony to how deeply committed he is to the life of the church and not merely the intrinsic good of scholarly output.

56. Lathrop, *Holy Things*, 7.

elements in worship yields a third reality, a new word that emerges from the placement of ancient symbols next to modern life, old stories and our own stories, ritual actions and biblical words. In this way, the power of old symbols, stories, and actions is broken and remade, now capable of speaking a new truth.[57] This pattern, Lathrop argues, is biblical, as we see in its treatment of everything from leavened bread[58] to Jesus Christ, who combines in himself the juxtaposition of messianic hope with the reality of an itinerant crucified as a zealot. In worship, too, our symbols are juxtaposed in a way to make new meaning. It is, Lathrop says, our own presence we bring into the sanctuary, our own water, and wine and bread around which we gather—and all these things have their own cluster of meanings. The meal we celebrate is the Feast of the Lamb, the Lord's Supper; the bath, a washing of sin and a dying and rising.

The things that are placed in juxtaposition are the "holy things" that are central to the church's worship: bath, book, table. "These are the basic things of the Christian community: water for washing, words for speaking and praying, a meal for eating."[59] There may be other symbols: people, space, time, cross, candle, oil—but these are subordinate to those central things, which speak of life and death in their symbolic richness. Lathrop then identifies other juxtapositions that speak their meanings into one another. The first important one is temporal: the week set next to the eighth day, a day "beyond the week, an opening to a thing the week cannot contain."[60] The second key juxtaposition is word and table, discourse and sign. Grounded in a *synaxis* service of the synagogue, the priestly sacrifices of the temple, and the communal meals of covenant and family, thanksgiving and generosity. This juxtaposition opens up meal and word and the life outside the sanctuary to new possibilities of grace and thanksgiving and justice.[61]

When Lathrop turns to matters of the church—in the second book of his trilogy, turning from liturgical theology to the more specific task of liturgical ecclesiology—he uses the same method, but now, the central symbol in view to be broken in its juxtaposition to other things is the worshipping assembly itself. All these "primary symbols of the faith communally

---

57. Lathrop, *Holy Things*, 27–31.
58. Lathrop, *Holy Things*, 24–27.
59. Lathrop, *Holy Things*, 103.
60. Lathrop, *Holy Things*, 40.
61. Lathrop, *Holy Things*, 47–51.

enacted" are done *as an assembly*.[62] It is the assembly that speaks, sings, and hears the Word, it is the assembly that bathes and welcomes, it is the assembly that feasts and remembers and prays. It is the assembly itself which is both "source and norm" for the theological method Lathrop employs in *Holy People*.[63] At the heart of this project, then, is the familiar insight and assertion that the church learns what it is when it is worshipping: "The assembly's identity is manifest—it is what it is—when it does the central things of Christian faith. If you will, the church begins to know itself not by contemplating its own identity, but by beholding the face of Christ in that word, bath, and table that manifest God's identity."[64] For Lathrop, then, liturgical ecclesiology is a "corollary" of liturgical theology, an attempt to see what the meaning of Christian worship says about the church: "The method of liturgical ecclesiology is the method of liturgy itself: meaning that occurs as one thing is put next to another in such a way that the community is called to faith in the Triune God."[65]

The first third of the book explains Lathrop's methodological approach, and then begins to construct a liturgical ecclesiology, exploring and critiquing "Assembly" as the central symbol. Key to Lathrop's method is to understand the church as fundamentally Eucharistic.[66] Liturgical ecclesiology, he writes, "needs to be 'consonant' with the Eucharist": turning the church not inward toward itself, but as itself looking outward, a "participant in God's life, and witness to God's love in the world."[67] Having the Eucharist at the center will give the church a foothold in finding its unity at the table amidst the diversity of worship practices the church knows. Yet he is not unaware that "Eucharist" means many things to many different communities, so he defines it rather broadly, in terms of juxtaposition: "A liturgical ecclesiology will need to accord with Eucharist, that is, with the entire economy of word and sacrament, of proclamation and thanksgiving,

---

62. Lathrop, *Holy People*, 8–9.

63. Saliers, "Review of *Holy People*," 30.

64. Lathrop, *Holy People*, 9. The footnote at this point significantly points to a passage in von Allmen that was quoted in Wainwright—a passage about the church learning who it is by looking at Christ's face.

65. Lathrop, *Holy People*, 14.

66. We will see that this adjective is central to von Allmen, too. In fact there are so many resonances and similarities between the two authors, we could exhaust ourselves identifying all of them.

67. Lathrop, *Holy People*, 15.

as that economy is present in all the churches."[68] Further, centering the assembly around the Eucharist brings a humility in the acknowledgment that it is only God who makes the church and makes it what it aspires to be: one, holy, and universal.

Lathrop's exploration of the "assembly" includes its typical characteristics, ways in which it is experienced as like or unlike other cultural assemblies, its individual and communal elements, and its eschatological significance. All of these things, says Lathrop—a Biblical name, images, practices, and faith—all juxtaposed, make a new thing: the church at worship.[69] His preliminary reflections conclude with a series of questions appropriate to a liturgical ecclesiology:

> How are such liturgical assemblies connected to a wider sense of "church"? What insights follow for the actual practice of assembly? Can the liturgy, conceived as the shared inheritance of the assemblies, indeed contribute to ecumenical unity? When we speak of "holy assembly," what do we actually mean by "holiness"? And if *ekklesia* always involves a crisis in our cultural conceptions of meeting, what insights can be drawn for the relationships between Christian worship and the cultures of the world?[70]

These questions are the very ones he explores in the remainder of the book, focusing in particular on the unity of persons within the Christian assembly and the links between them and other assemblies; and, in the last third of the book, the relationship between the assembly and the culture around it along with the cultural patterns of meaning that surround it.

These questions might all be properly located under rubrics drawn from the Nicene marks of the church, explorations of the church as one, holy, catholic, and apostolic. These four are central to Lathrop's liturgical ecclesiology, though he does not put them front-and-center organizationally. Yet from the outset, he argues that "catholicity, unity, and holiness are intrinsic to the Gospel of Jesus Christ, who calls the apostolic worshiping/serving community into being."[71] Not only are they intrinsic to the Gospel, which calls the church into being, they are intrinsic to the church at its most churchly—the worshipping assembly. Don Saliers notes that for other theologians, these notes have often been used without much reference to wor-

68. Lathrop, *Holy People*, 16.
69. Lathrop, *Holy People*, 40.
70. Lathrop, *Holy People*, 48.
71. Saliers, "Review of *Holy People*," 30.

ship. But Lathrop takes them, adds to them other ecclesial characteristics (e.g., Martin Luther's seven tangible marks[72]), and explores their *liturgical* significance. These creedal marks are both descriptive of any Christian assembly and, at the same time, aspirational descriptors of what the church might be or become. They are both descriptive and prescriptive.[73]

> The assemblies in many different places are *one* because they are gathered into the life of the one triune God by the use of one Baptism, the hearing of one Word, the celebration of one table. Those same assemblies are *holy* because they are being called as the holy assembly of scriptural promise by that Word of God they are hearing and because, in their nakedness and need, in their union with all the needy people of the earth, they are eating and drinking and speaking to each other the very forgiveness of God. The assemblies are the *catholic* church because they do these things in ever new cultural situations, according to the dignity of each local place, bringing the gifts of lands and peoples into the unity that links all the assemblies across time and space. And the assemblies are *apostolic* because there reverberates, as the assembly's central meaning in the midst of all these marks of their life, the apostolic witness, made with apostolic, God-sent, authority, that Christ is risen and that in his resurrection all things are becoming new.[74]

Though absent a creedal list or some other widely accepted list of ecclesial activities, Lathrop offers reflection on what it is the church *does*, in addition to what the church *is*. But since his definition of church is centered on its worshipping activities, Lathrop's focus is on activities such as preaching, teaching, and celebration of the sacraments. He does speak of other things that are central to the church's ministry: welcoming the stranger, demonstrating love, generous sharing of gifts, etc. As with the Nicene marks, he links these closely to the church's defining activity of worship.

72. Saliers, "Review of *Holy People*," 31. See also Lathrop, *Holy People*, 54–62.

73. Lathrop, *Holy People*, 79.

74. Lathrop, *Holy People*, 56. See also Lathrop, *Holy People*, 58–64. Lathrop explores the marks of the church even more thoroughly in a follow-up work of liturgical ecclesiology, *Christian Assembly: Marks of the Church in a Pluralistic Age*. In that (very Lutheran) work, he explores the use of the marks as descriptive tags, as a way to discern the authenticity of a Christian community, as liturgical lodestars, and as aids for congregations to evaluate themselves and their leadership.

Thus, hospitality, up-building, koinonia,[75] and even structures of leadership are first encountered and expressed in worship.[76]

These features of Lathrop's liturgical ecclesiology will guide our own articulation of a liturgical ecclesiology in the writings of Jean-Jacques von Allmen. Lathrop's starting point is a working assumption that the worshipping assembly is definitive of what the church is. He asserts that this assembly gathers fundamentally around word and table together, and that both its activity and its identity are found here. In addition, Lathrop's theological reflections as secondary liturgical ecclesiology turn—in both descriptive and prescriptive ways—to reform of the church's worshipping practices in a practically-applied "pastoral" liturgical ecclesiology. The question "what is church" is answered, for Lathrop, by looking at the worshipping assembly:

> Perhaps an approach to church by way of the concrete answers of the liturgical assembly of Christians will be able to unite certain strengths of these answers, holding the answers together, making them available to each other and to us all. Further, perhaps a liturgical ecclesiology can avoid something of the weaknesses of these answers, the ways in which our own community or an idealized community or my own taste in communities can be put too easily at the heart of a definition of "church."[77]

MATTHIJS PLOEGER

Other scholars are now emerging who confirm von Allmen's—and subsequently Lathrop's—methodological move, following them by either discerning or constructing a liturgical ecclesiology. One such scholar is the Roman Catholic priest Mattijs Ploeger. His published dissertation, a lengthy and sweeping work, *Celebrating Church: Ecumenical Contributions to a Liturgical Ecclesiology*, begins at the same starting place that von Allmen and Lathrop do, locating the source of ecclesiological reflection in the church at worship: "How does it affect one's ecclesiology, if one takes the liturgical—particularly the Eucharistic—celebration as the central ecclesial event?" He then surveys a large sample of ecumenically representative theologians (including von Allmen) to discern the liturgical ecclesiology

75. Lathrop has a section of the book explicitly devoted to *koinonia*. See Lathrop, *Holy Things*, 120–30.

76. Lathrop, *Holy Things*, 6.

77. Lathrop, *Holy Things*, 6.

embedded in their work. We will briefly explore the method Ploeger uses and the synthetic conclusions to which he comes, and then examine, in more detail, the liturgical ecclesiology Ploeger sees in von Allmen.

The investigation Ploeger initiates in this work is self-consciously one of systematic theology. That is to say, the data he surveys is the systematic theological work of other scholars, and he intends his conclusions to be primarily systematic-theological.[78] In doing this, he contrasts with Lathrop, who does indeed engage in systematic work, but also takes a 'pastoral' turn at the end of each section of his books, offering suggestions for reforming present practice. Furthermore, Lathrop is a *constructive* liturgical ecclesiologist, as his sources are his own richly understood sense of the assembly and its central purposes. Ploeger, on the other hand, is a *comparative* ecclesiologist, looking at the writings of representative theologians from a variety of ecclesial traditions, as well as a selection of relevant texts from projects of ecumenical dialogue.

Ploeger recognizes that the phrase "Liturgical Ecclesiology" is a rather new one, and says that for him, the term is a contraction of two terms that together locate his work at the intersection of "Eucharistic ecclesiology" and "liturgical theology."[79] His discussion of the latter term offers a review of the history of the liturgical movement, identifying its four "pillars": history, theology, practice, and ritual studies. He reviews some of the main liturgical theologians of the past century, coming to the conclusion that a clearly-defined relationship between *theologia prima* and *theologia secunda*, between *lex orandi* and *lex credendi,* may not be possible. But "however one defines the discipline and method of liturgical theology, there is always—implicitly or explicitly—a mutual interaction between theology and liturgy."[80] His survey of ecclesiology notes that it, too, has been practiced in various modes: biblical, historical, systematic and practical. His focus will be on "Eucharistic" ecclesiology, drawing on Walter Kasper's work, summarized in the phrase *Ubi eucharistic, ibi ecclesia.*[81] Ploeger, however, hopes to draw the circle a bit wider, and when he speaks of "Eucharistic ecclesiology" he means to have the church's entire liturgical celebration in view. The

---

78. Ploeger, *Celebrating Church*, 4.

79. Ploeger, *Celebrating Church*, 5.

80. Ploeger, *Celebrating Church*, 16.

81. Ploeger, *Celebrating Church*, 19.

Eucharist, he says, is the "kernel" of the liturgy, but not all of it. "All that the church does is summarized in, but not swallowed up by the Eucharist."[82]

At the intersection of these two fields, then, Ploeger explicitly borrows Lathrop's phrase to name his present project (though he traces its etymology differently):

> The value of the phrase "liturgical ecclesiology" is that the attention is not exclusively focused on the Eucharist, but also on the very act of the gathering (important in view of the *ekklesia*) and on the juxtapositions of which the liturgy consists (important in view of the liturgy conveying Christian meaning).[83]

Beyond the liturgical celebration itself, Ploeger is interested in exploring how a liturgical ecclesiology might say something about the liturgy after the liturgy, the life of the worshipping church in its everyday existence. A liturgical ecclesiology, he says, will have something to say about doxological living and Eucharistic ethics. "Liturgical ecclesiology investigates the ecclesial character of the liturgy, which includes the gathering of the members of the church, prayer, song, baptism, the Word, the Eucharist, and its implications for daily life in and outside the church, and all those other 'juxtapositions' which make Christian liturgy what it is."[84]

After this methodological overview, the bulk of Ploeger's book is taken up with a comprehensive survey of theologians, five or six each from the major church traditions: Orthodox, Roman Catholic, Old Catholic, Anglican and Protestant.[85] Notable figures include John Zizioulas, Henri DeLubac, Joseph Ratzinger, Andreas Rinkel, Kurt Stalder, Gregory Dix, Catharine Pickstock, Geoffrey Wainwright, Jean-Jacques von Allmen, and Gordon Lathrop. He also includes an additional chapter examining some key texts from ecumenical efforts (*Baptism, Eucharist and Ministry*, for instance). He concludes with a synthetic summary of his findings.

In that summary Ploeger identifies a few of the central and common features of an ecumenical liturgical ecclesiology. Among those features is an accounting for the connection between Jesus Christ, the Holy Spirit, and

---

82. Ploeger, *Celebrating Church*, 20.

83. Ploeger, *Celebrating Church*, 21.

84. Ploeger, *Celebrating Church*, 22.

85. It is interesting that here he distinguishes Roman Catholic from "Old Catholic" and has just one chapter to encompass all the non-Anglican Protestants, using Wainwright, Lathrop, and von Allmen as the main voices representing, respectively, the Methodist, the Lutheran, and the Reformed traditions.

the church, and an understanding of why "baptism, Eucharist, and the wider liturgy are constitutive for the Christian faith and church."[86] But at the heart of it, for Ploeger, is "the biblical-theological concept of *koinonia*."[87] Ploeger has in mind here not a shallow sense of mere "fellowship" or coffee-klatch conviviality. He articulates instead a robust sense of communal participation that is Trinitarian, anthropological, soteriological, ecclesiological, and Eucharistic. It begins with the perichoretic *koinonia* of the Trinity. Human beings, made in God's image, share in this relationality, destined both for communion with one another and participation in God's Trinitarian love. Salvation is then understood as the restoration of right relations, of communion. And the church, as a means of grace and an instrument in God's salvation plan, is a provisional, imperfect, and yet "tangible community of redeemed divine-human and inter-human relationality."[88] The Eucharist (broadly construed) becomes the paradigm of *koinonia* as the members of the assembly "have *koinonia* with one another through their corporate *koinonia* with Jesus Christ and through him with God."[89]

In addition Ploeger addresses in his summary some "sub-questions" concerning ordained ministry and the local-universal dialectic, two topics that many ecclesiologists put front and center in their work, but which have less obvious liturgical connections. Finally, Ploeger articulates the relationship between the liturgical life of the church and its other activities—pastoral, diaconal, catechetical, and organizational. A liturgical ecclesiology, he says, takes the liturgy as *paradigmatic* for what the church most essentially is. But this is "not synonymous with saying that celebrating the liturgy is enough for being church or that all other ecclesial activities stand in the shadow of the liturgy."[90] Instead, the liturgy creates a "centrifugal center" by which the church is sent out to the world as a result of its encounter in worship. The Eucharist "generates mission by its proleptical character and determines ethics by its *koinonia* character."[91]

Summary. Mattaijs Ploeger, explicitly following the methodological trail blazed by Jean-Jacques von Allmen and paved by Gordon Lathrop, has articulated a type of ecumenical liturgical ecclesiology. He does so by

---

86. Ploeger, *Celebrating Church*, 457.
87. Ploeger, *Celebrating Church*, 459.
88. Ploeger, *Celebrating Church*, 463.
89. Ploeger, *Celebrating Church*, 467.
90. Ploeger, *Celebrating Church*, 528–29.
91. Ploeger, *Celebrating Church*, 539.

comparing the ecclesiologies he finds in the liturgical theology of a wide range of ecumenical scholars. In contrast to many other ecclesiologists we have surveyed, Ploeger does not structure his synthesis around the Nicene marks or give them significant organizational weight;[92] instead, he centers his work on the concept of *koinonia*, which is, for him, at the heart of the worshipping church.[93] The other activities of the church then flow from this center.

Ploeger on Jean-Jacques von Allmen

Jean-Jacques von Allmen is among the theologians upon whose work Ploeger bases his synthesis. We now turn to Ploeger's explicit treatment of von Allmen's liturgical ecclesiology. Because we will articulate the content of von Allmen's liturgical ecclesiology in some depth later, our summary of Ploeger's work with von Allmen will be brief, highlighting his methodological choices.

Jean-Jacques von Allmen was a prolific scholar, writing hundreds of essays in the course of his career.[94] To make his study manageable, Ploeger identified three of von Allmen's most significant works and focused his efforts there. The books he chose were: *Célébrer le Salut* (English translation: *Worship: Its Theory and Practice*); *Essai sur le reps du Seigneur* (English translation: *The Lord's Supper*); and *Prophétisme Sacramentel*. The first two are well-known and the last is a collection of essays on a number of topics— both liturgical and ecclesial—that were previously published in academic journals. When undertaking a project like this, the choice to narrow the material in view makes sense. I find puzzling, however, his decision not to engage von Allmen's primary work on baptism (*Pastorale du Baptême*), nor his foundational work on the proclamation of the Word, *Preaching and Congregation*. This last omission seems especially significant, as we will see below.

---

92. Of course, the marks are still in view; Ploeger's interest in the universal/local dynamic of the church is a riff on its unity and catholicity.

93. Interestingly, Ploeger offers a kind of supplemental justification for this approach in the ambiguity of the Latin phrase *sanctorum communionem* in the Apostles' Creed. Normally translated "communion of the saints," it may also be fairly translated "participation in the holy things," pointing likely to the Eucharist. See Ploeger, *Celebrating Church*, 19.

94. See Bobrinskoy et al., "Bibliographie J.-J. von Allmen," 1–17.

Ploeger names a handful of themes that are central to von Allmen's liturgical ecclesiology. Though he does not identify them as such, the ones he picks are—characteristic for von Allmen—dialectic in nature.[95] For example, Ploeger identifies von Allmen's ecumenical impulse as a central theme. As a self-conscious and self-critical Reformed Protestant, von Allmen insisted that his own church should always strive to uphold the orthodox faith and be part of the Catholic Church. He was, therefore, often seen by those in his own tribe as "catholicizing" and by his Roman dialogue partners as an "always reforming" reformer.[96]

Another theme Ploeger identifies as central to von Allmen's liturgical ecclesiology is the inseparable unity of word and sacrament. Here, he points even to the title of von Allmen's collection of essays, *Prophétisme sacramentel*. Sacraments, argues von Allmen, are prophetic in that they imply both threat and promise; and preaching is sacramental because it makes present what it proclaims.[97] Ploeger rightly points to von Allmen's insistence that the Eucharist is central to the liturgy and constitutive of the church. Yet von Allmen would be quick to insist, with equal vehemence, on the centrality of preaching for worship—preaching that offers a dialectical counterpoint to the Eucharist so that worship maintains its eschatological tension between the already-realized kingdom, anticipated and tasted in the Supper, and the not-yet-but-someday-soon kingdom toward which the proclaimed Word points and directs and encourages. Ploeger sees that preaching is important for von Allmen, but it warrants little more than a footnote in his exploration of von Allmen's liturgical ecclesiology.[98]

Another central dialectic in view for Ploeger in von Allmen is the eschatological tension that characterizes the church's place in the world. The church is the realm in which God's future is made present by the Spirit. Thus, the church is both critical of and affirmative of the world. Baptism is the threshold of access to the table, the place where the world must give up its life for the sake of finding it again in Christ. The church is both in the realm of the coming kingdom and in that kingdom's prefiguration in this very world. It is both distinct from the world and it is the first fruits of its

95. For example, in *Lord's Supper*, von Allmen treats the topic in six chapters, each of which looks at the sacrament through a dialectical lens; for example, Eucharist as revelation of both the limitations and plenitude of the church; Prayer and Fulfillment; Communion with Christ and with the Brethren.

96. Ploeger, *Celebrating Church*, 334.

97. Ploeger, *Celebrating Church*, 335.

98. Ploeger, *Celebrating Church*, 340n19.

restoration; that is the nature of its holiness. Its task, then, is to be a sign of God's intention and a tool of God's activity to bring the whole world back to its real meaning and doxological purpose.[99]

Among the classic ecclesiological dialectics that Ploeger explores in von Allmen is the church's character as both local and universal. The church "has to be a genuine representation of the (many) varieties in the world, while at the same time being a prefiguration of the (one) kingdom."[100] This dual nature is most true and most clearly seen when the Eucharist is celebrated. The fullness of the church is present in every local Eucharistic community. Only a local church celebrates Communion, but it is connected to *every* church that celebrates Communion, because they have Communion with the same Christ present at the meal.[101]

Ploeger takes note of von Allmen's "predilection for nuptial imagery"[102] when speaking of the church, but spends more time exploring the dialectic at the heart of von Allmen's favorite image for worship: a beating heart. Here, von Allmen sets in juxtaposition the Lord's Day with the other days of the week and the ministry carried out by the church. The church assembles on Sunday for the Eucharistic liturgy just as the blood comes into the heart in the diastole movement, and then is sent forth in the systole to service and mission in the world.

Finally, Ploeger explores a few dialectic distinctions related to the apostolicity of the church and its ordained ministry. There is, first of all, the distinction between the priestly and ministerial roles of those in the assembly. The former belongs to all those who are baptized. The latter is reserved for those who have been ordained to represent Christ to his people. Both roles are necessary—shepherd and flock, father and family, groom and bride, visitor and visited. Thus, all elements of ecclesiastical structure and organization must have a relationship to the Eucharistic gathering. Second, with regards specifically to apostolic succession, von Allmen distinguishes between pastoral succession and doctrinal succession. These are normally held together, but the former was abandoned at the Reformation

99. Ploeger, *Celebrating Church*, 347.

100. Ploeger, *Celebrating Church*, 337.

101. This same logic might be extended to the proclamation of the Word, as von Allmen does in *Preaching & Congregation*.

102. Ploeger, *Celebrating Church*, 341.

by Protestants in order to hold on to the latter. And now, the exceptional situation that resulted has become lamentably ordinary.[103]

Ploeger's treatment of von Allmen (and the other figures he discusses) is focused on a "systematic-theological" liturgical ecclesiology. Thus, he does not spend much time offering any of what Lathrop would call "pastoral" liturgical ecclesiology—i.e., reflection with a reforming edge for the church's practice. Neither does he examine the sections of von Allmen's writings where von Allmen engages in these practical reflections. One key exception is his notation of von Allmen's strong critique of both Protestant and Roman Catholic traditions regarding the Eucharist. The Roman Church is faulted for not letting the whole congregation receive Communion under both species at each celebration of the Eucharist. Protestants are faulted for not celebrating the Eucharist each Lord's Day. "Either way, the baptized are deprived of their full participation in the weekly Eucharist and thus, treated as catechumens."[104]

Summary. Mattaijs Ploeger's reading of Jean-Jacques von Allmen focuses on three central works and a handful of important themes, often articulated in a dialectical way. Though he has some concern for the pastoral or practical, his primary interest is in discerning and articulating a coherent, systematic liturgical ecclesiology. He does not offer much exploration of von Allmen's treatment of the church's "post-liturgy" or "diastole" activities, such as mission or service. And though he does not make organizational use of the Nicene marks, the themes and issues he does identify as important in von Allmen's writing are closely caught up in them: the church's unity in relation to its universality, its holiness in relation to the rest of the world, and its apostolic identity in concern for the ordained ministry.

PLANS AND MATERIALS

Up to this point, we have been trying to provide fairly fine-grained methodological context for an examination of Jean-Jacques von Allmen's liturgical ecclesiology. We have noted that liturgical ecclesiology is itself a relatively new term, and a relatively new sub-sub-sub-discipline in the field of theology. Yet some noteworthy settlers followed von Allmen's precedent, demonstrating the value of doing this new thing called liturgical ecclesiology. The work in the pages that follow will join Mitchell, Wainwright, Chan,

103. Ploeger, *Celebrating Church*, 344–47.
104. Ploeger, *Celebrating Church*, 342.

Lathrop, Ploeger, and others in the place where church and worship are juxtaposed.

Our method vis-à-vis *liturgical theology* will be to take a cue from von Allmen, recognizing the complex and reciprocal relationship of the church's *orandi* and *credendi*. Thus, in chapters 3 and 4, we will summarize von Allmen as he speaks of the church at worship in both prescriptive and descriptive modes. Likewise, when we turn to 'pastoral' liturgical ecclesiology in chapter 5, and we explore some implications for liturgical and homiletical practice derived from von Allmen's 'secondary' liturgical ecclesiology, the suggestions we make will come in both descriptive and prescriptive modes, addressing problems both general and contextually specific.

Our method vis-à-vis *ecclesiology* is to put on the spectacles of Nicene ecclesiology—the four identifying marks of the church—and to look at von Allmen's liturgical theology through them.[105] However, one could also understand this metaphor in the reverse: this project will look at the Nicene marks (as explored in von Allmen's liturgical theology) through liturgical lenses, making clearer what is already implicit there.[106] We do so with the purpose of showing von Allmen's usefulness as a conversation partner—both for ecclesiologists and for liturgical theologians. A secondary purpose is to demonstrate how a worship-centered ecclesiology might offer practical and pastoral guidance for contemporary problems of the worshipping church, such as regular baptismal remembrance, fencing the table, the shape of the evangelical worship order, sacramental preaching, and the evaluation of worship.

Our approach going forward will be as follows. Chapters 3 and 4 will examine selected writings of liturgical theology from Jean-Jacques von Allmen, using patterns and paradigms borrowed from ecclesiology—namely, descriptive terms that point to the church's fundamental identity. Chapter 5 will then articulate a few implications this liturgical ecclesiology may have for reforming the practice of both preaching and worship. But first, in chapter 2, we turn to a brief biography of Jean-Jacques von Allmen to put his work into a fitting *historical* context.

---

105. Like Ploeger, our explorations will be delimited to a select number of von Allmen's many works. Secondary sources will make an appearance as necessary, but the primary sources will be von Allmen's fundamental works of liturgical theology, using the English translations where possible. These are: *Worship: Its Theology & Practice; Preaching and Congregation; The Lord's Supper;* and *Pastorale du baptême.*

106. My gratitude to Martha Moore-Keish for pointing this out in an earlier draft.

CHAPTER 2

Jean-Jacques von Allmen, Biography

[In his writings], Jean-Jacques von Allmen has been able to pass on that which made up his life, that which his students at Neuchâtel and elsewhere so enjoyed from the master, that which his colleagues and friends must owe him—something firmer, deeper, more sustainable—a vision of Christian worship based on the immense love of Christ and the Church.

—JACQUES LEMOINE[1]

THE LIFE AND WORK of Jean-Jacques von Allmen was devoted to and shaped by the two central ecclesial developments of the twentieth century: the ecumenical movement and the liturgical renewal movement. His pastoral work, his scholarly writing, and his participation in the broader church all demonstrate his dual passion for the unity of the church and the revitalization of its worship. Bruno Bürki, one of von Allmen's students, wrote that the goal pursued by von Allmen throughout all his works was to push for a "courageous reform of the Church of Christ for the re-establishment of the church's unity."[2] This brief biographical sketch will review von Allmen's life in pursuit of these two passions and testify to the fruit it bore.

1. Lemoine, "Célébrer," 53. "Von Allmen a su faire passer ce qui fait sa vie, ce que ses étudiants de Neuchâtel et d'ailleurs ont tant apprécié auprès du maître, ce que ses collègues et ses amis lui doivent de plus ferme, de plus profond, de plus durable: une vision de culte chrétien fondée sur un immense amour du Christ et de l'Église."

2. Bürki, "Jean-Jacques von Allmen," 52.

THE STUDENT

Jean-Jacques von Allmen was born on July 29, 1917, in Lausanne, Switzerland, to a devout family. His father, a chemist by profession, was originally from Neuchâtel, but took a job in Basel in 1918 and moved the family with him. His childhood and adolescence were spent there. Jean-Jacques von Allmen was baptized in 1933, at the end of a catechism course, as was the Swiss custom. In 1935, after completing his undergraduate education, he followed another Swiss custom by spending a gap year in England to complement his German and French language skills with a more solid grasp of English.

That year, at least parts of Switzerland were abuzz with the news that Karl Barth was returning to Basel from Nazi Germany. Jean-Jacques von Allmen was eager to study with Barth. But in the fall of 1936, he enrolled and began his studies with the Faculty of Theology of the Evangelical Free Church of the Canton of Vaud in Lausanne. He went to his birth town rather than Basel, in part because his mother held the "Cedar House" in high regard. The Cedar House was a small faculty established at the Free University in 1847. It had established a reputation as a serious institution, with academically excellent teaching and theological formation.[3]

His class was small: only eight students. But significantly, among von Allmen's peers and friends was Roger Schutz, who would later become the founder and first prior of the influential Taizé ecumenical community in France. This was the beginning of a long and mutually appreciative relationship between the two.

One significant experience that colored von Allmen's formation and future trajectory was his participation in the Second World Conference on Faith and Order in Edinburgh in August 1937. He was probably the youngest delegate present, and he was dazzled by people of denominations other than his own. He made friendships that would sustain him throughout his life, and established partnerships in the ecumenical efforts that would

---

The sources for biographical information about von Allmen are primarily in French. For the purposes of this book, when I cite these sources, I will keep the body text in English. The translations, unless otherwise noted, are my own. I will not footnote every fact, but will do so where appropriate, as when an authority draws an interpretive conclusion, or when a turn of phrase is particularly felicitous. I acknowledge my indebtedness to the following articles: Bridel, "la passion de unite," 561–75; Montmollin, "Jean-Jacques von Allmen," 315–18; and Haquin, "Les sacrements de l'initiation chrétienne," 135–50.

3 Bridel, "la passion de unite," 562.

characterize his later years. His participation in this event was followed by attending the World Conference of Christian Youth in Amsterdam in August 1939, where those present engaged in global reflection on ecumenism in what one biographer calls a "twilight atmosphere"—with the shadow of the German threat hanging over the event.

In the middle of his educational program, von Allmen moved to Basel to continue his studies there, where he spent two years learning from (among others) Karl Barth and Oscar Cullman, the most influential voices in the development of von Allmen's theology. He learned his approach to scripture (particularly the New Testament) from Cullman, his approach to practical theology from Jean-Louis Leuba and Emil Brunner, and he read and re-read the texts of the sixteenth century reformers to detect traces of an awareness of the catholicity of the church. In his later years, it was the theological vitality of Barth that encouraged von Allmen to extend certain themes into ecclesiological and ecumenical fields.[4]

In addition to his studies, von Allmen became involved with the Christian Student Association. He was invited by Leuba to become a member of the editorial board of the magazine *In Extremis*. There, he was responsible for heading the news and information from the Student Association. He wrote other features, too, including a well-received and high-spirited article on his favorite poet, C. F. Ramuz, in which he celebrated what he called the "dear Barthism of Ramuz! Milk and honey for dialecticians!"[5] Many attribute his charming writing style and frequently poetic sense of form to the influence of Ramuz's poetry.[6]

When the mobilization came for the war, Barth took up his part with his contemporaries. He alternated between serving his country as a soldier (for the neutral Switzerland) and turning his regular off-duty leaves into fruitful holidays, in which he would write both for his classes and articles for *In Extremis*.

Jean-Jacques von Allmen spent the prescribed semester at the University of Neuchâtel and graduated in the spring of 1941. He married Alice Tissot of Colombier in June of that same year, and in July, he was

4. According to one of his doctoral students, Hughes Oliphant Old, it was more Barth's theological vitality than any particular theological position that charged von Allmen's work. Cullman, Old says, was more influential in the development of von Allmen's ecclesiology. See Old, "Reminiscences and Reflections."

5. von Allmen, *In Extremis*, 57.

6. Bridel, "la passion de unite," 566.

dedicated to pastoral ministry in Boudevilliers, a municipality in the canton of Neuchâtel.

THE PASTOR

Jean-Jacques von Allmen had prepared to be a pastor, not a professor. He exercised what he considered this "essential" ministry with enthusiasm and joy for seventeen years, from 1941 to 1958. Unlike many of his colleagues, he never considered the pastorate as a stepping stone to academic heights. Bridel characterized his whole theological corpus as an encouragement and "exhortation to his brothers and pastors, among whose company he would have liked to stay."[7]

Very little is written about von Allmen's day-to-day pastoral work in these years. Yet the scholarly themes we will see articulated later reflect not only the energizing theology of Karl Barth but also the ordinary concerns of a pastor who has to preach and lead worship each Lord's Day, and who has to engage daily with an increasingly pluralistic and secular culture for whom the disunity of the church is a scandal. It is not too much to say that his liturgical theology emerged from boots-on-the-ground ecclesiological experience as a parish pastor.

He began his pastoral service at Val de Travers, in the canton of Neuchâtel, among young, Swiss, German-speaking immigrants, from 1941 until 1943. He then served a church in Ponts de Martel, the French church of Lucerne.

These years were exciting ones for von Allmen. The previous decade had seen a renewal in the life and thought of all reformed churches, thanks in large measure to Karl Barth and his dialectical theology.[8] In addition, the Neuchâtel Reformed Church reconstituted its unity—after seventy years of separation—in 1938. This offered a small taste of success for those who long sought unity, and in the years that followed, it provided an enlarged field for his ministry and teaching.[9]

Throughout the war years, Switzerland had been, in many ways, cut off from the international contacts that had previously fed its cultural life. Nevertheless, as a young ecumenist, von Allmen developed relationships beyond the parochial circles in which he ministered. His growing friendship

7. Bridel, "la passion de unite," 564.
8. Montmollin, "Jean-Jacques von Allmen," 316.
9. Senn, "Worship, Doctrine, and Life," 454.

with Barth was one such relationship, but many foreign theologians took visits in Switzerland that were more or less illegal, and von Allmen made the most of these opportunities.[10] Additionally, during his years in Lucerne as the pastor of the French church, von Allmen was able to make his first discovery of Catholicism by frequently visiting professors and making friends among the faculty of theology there.

In 1945, he began work on his PhD at the University of Neuchâtel. He received his doctorate in 1948 and resumed his work in the pastorate in Lucerne until 1954. Then, he moved to Lignières until 1958. In that year, he accepted a position as professor of practical theology at the University of Neuchâtel, where his inaugural lecture, "The Holy Spirit and Worship," testified to his love for pastoral ministry, as it explores the mystery of the church as the perpetually re-actualized work of the Holy Spirit.

THE PUBLISHER

In addition to his pastoral duties, von Allmen was often found during these years pen in hand, either writing or editing the work of others.

In 1944 he published a French translation of the *Heidelberg Catechism* (the first in forty years), and in 1945, a translation of *Ministère de l'intercession* by Hans Asmussen. In 1948, he contributed a translation of the famous essay by Oscar Cullman on *Le baptême des infants et la doctrine biblique du baptême*. Another important work produced during the years of his pastoral ministry was the reflective and aptly-titled *La Vie Pastorale* (The Pastoral Life) in 1956. He also edited and wrote several articles for the highly esteemed *Vocabulaire biblique* (translated quickly into English), and in 1958, pursued a *ressourcement* of sorts—an adapted and enhanced recovery of the Heidelberg Catechism entitled *Appartenir à Jésus-Christ* (Belonging to Jesus Christ). All these works appeared in one theological collection or another, created under his impetus through the Neuchâtelois publisher "Delachaux and Niestlé," with whom he developed and sustained a prolonged and fruitful relationship, becoming secretary of their theological collections in the late 40s.

Of course, this truncated list does not include his most important work of these years: his doctoral dissertation, published in 1947, but submitted early in 1948 to the faculty of Theology of the University of Neuchâtel. The dissertation—*L'Eglise et ses functions d'après Jean-Frédéric Ostervald*—was

10. Bridel, "la passion de unite," 565.

dedicated to its subject, von Allmen's eighteenth-century predecessor in the training of clergy in Neuchâtel. Ostervald's work was characterized, like von Allmen's, by a desire to reform the worship of the church, and through it, to achieve a confessional rapprochement: "Ostervald tried . . . to reform the Neuchâtel church and to thus participate with a more general reformation of all the European churches."[11]

The thesis is divided into two parts, one dealing with the character or *identity* of the church, the other with the ministry or *functions* of the church. With regard to the church's identity, von Allmen stresses the importance for Ostervald of other denominations. In fact, Ostervald is very much like von Allmen in that he did not hide his attraction to Anglicanism. "In the Church of England, Ostervald saw a form of the global church which all Christians could join. She reflected the true image of the universal Church—having no pope, and during the Reformation, keeping everything that could be preserved."[12] At the same time, von Allmen is more critical of Ostervald in the second section, citing his moralism with regard to the Lord's Supper, and commenting that he "likes to talk about the struggle against ignorance more than he likes to talk about the truth."[13]

Jean-Jacques von Allmen's dissertation appeared in 1947 as Occasional Paper No. 3 of the "Theological Papers of the Protestant News," published by Delachaux and Niestlé. The years that followed were productive for von Allmen. But he was not content to publish only his own works. For twenty years, he animated this publishing house, was its full-time secretary from 1946–1948, and along with his *In Extremis* partner, Jean-Louis Leuba, launched *The Theological Papers* (*La Caheirs Theologique*) in 1943. These papers include more than sixty issues, featuring the most notable theologians of the time. The first two, in fact, are by von Allmen's seminary heroes, Oscar Cullmann and Karl Barth. In addition, von Allmen was an editor of the ecumenical journal *Verbum Caro*, published out of Taizé, for years—a journal to which he contributed many significant articles.

THE PROFESSOR

In 1958, von Allmen was appointed to the chair of practical theology at the University of Neuchâtel. He remained there until his retirement in 1980.

11. von Allmen, "L'actualité de J.F. Ostervald, 65.

12. von Allmen, *L'Eglise et ses fonctions*, 48–49.

13. von Allmen, *L'Eglise et ses fonctions*, 65.

He was made assistant dean in 1961, dean of the faculty in 1963, and Vice-Chancellor in 1969. In 1971 he took part-time duties at the University until 1974 in order to help found the Tantur Institute in Jerusalem (about which more is below).

Despite these administrative responsibilities, von Allmen was active and productive in many ways. He maintained an ongoing relationship with local churches, preaching regularly and leading catechism classes and other small study groups. He traveled to many countries as a regular contributor to the Faith & Order Commission of the Ecumenical Council of the WCC and as a member and president of *Societas Liturgica*. In addition, by all accounts, von Allmen gave vigilant attention to his students. His lectures were clear, his insight visionary, and his passion contagious.[14] The work of his most notable doctoral students we have already hinted at in the footnotes, including scholars such as Bruno Bürki, Boris Bobrinskoy, and Hughes Oliphant Old, not to mention scholars such as Geoffrey Wainwright, who served with von Allmen on the Faith and Order Commission of the World Council of Churches and has translated some of his best articles for the English-speaking world. Finally, in addition to all of this, von Allmen was an extraordinarily productive scholar during these years, writing more than a dozen books and 100 articles. The list of authors who were eager to contribute to the 1982 *festschrift* in his honor attests to the regard with which he was held.[15]

Of course, much of von Allmen's writing deals directly with topics in our line of sight: worship renewal and ecumenism. But beyond these topics, von Allmen wrote widely and deeply in the field of practical theology. A selective bibliography would include at least these works:

- "L'Ascension." In *Les étapes de l'an de grace, ouvrage collectif*, 87–106. Neuchâtel et Paris: Delachaux & Niestlé, 1962.

- *Prophétisme Sacramentel: Neuf études sur le renouveau et l'unité de l'Eglise*. Neuchâtel et Paris: Delachaux & Niestlé, 1964.

- "Clergé et laïcat." In *Verbum Caro*, 88–118. Taize, 1964.

- "A Short Theology of the Place of Worship." *Studia Liturgica* (1964) 155–71.

14. Bridel, "la passion de unite," 565. It is worth noting that one of the books at the heart of this study—von Allmen's *Worship: Its Theology and Practice*—is an edited translation of the lecture notes he offered in his Neuchâtel University course on worship.

15. See Bobrinskoy, *Communio Sanctorum*.

- "Réflexions d'un Protestant sur le pédobaptisme généralisé." *La Maison-Dieu, revue de pastoral liturgique* 89.1 (1967) 66–86.

- "Le Saint Ministère selon la conviction et la volonté des Réformés du XVIe siècle." In *Bibliothèque Théologique*. Neuchâtel et Paris: Delachaux & Niestlé, 1968.

- "The Theological Frame of a Liturgical Renewal." *The Church Quarterly* 2.1 (1969) 8–23.

- "La nécessité de l'Eglise pour la mission." *Parole et Mission, revue de thèologie missionnaire* 13.48 (1970) 59–70.

- "Une réforme dans l'Eglise, possibilité, critères, auteurs, étapes." In Vol. 1 of *Recherches et Synthéses d'Oecuménisme*. Gembloux: Ducolot, 1971.

- "The Theological Meaning of Common Prayer." *Studia Liturgica* 10.3/4 (1974) 125–36.

- "La primauté de l'Eglise de Pierre et du Paul: remarques d'un Protestant." In *Cahiers oecuméniques* 10. Paris: Editions du Cerf, 1977.

- "Le caractère communautaire du culte réformé" in *L'assemblée liturgique et les différent roles dans l'assemblée, Conférences St. Serge, XXIIIe semaine d'études liturgiques, paris, 28 juin–1er juillet 1976, Edizioni liturgiche, Via Pompeo Magno* 21 (1977) 11–23.

- "Les marques de l'Eglise." *RThPh* 113.2 (1982) 97–107.

THE REFORMER

In 1958, when Jean-Jacques von Allmen took up the position as professor of practical theology at the University of Neuchâtel, his inaugural lecture was on the topic of "The Holy Spirit and Worship." Von Allmen was always keenly interested in issues surrounding the church at worship, and his four most significant works—the works that resource our articulation of von Allmen's liturgical ecclesiology in the next chapter—deal centrally with this defining ecclesial activity. Like his liturgical forbearer John Calvin, von Allmen sees the Holy Spirit as the animating force in the church's worship, and the source of its renewal.

It is likely that von Allmen's most influential work is the publication of his liturgy course notes from 1960–61, initially published in French,[16] but quickly translated into English by Fletcher Fleet and published through Oxford early in his career (1965) as *Worship: Its Theology and Practice.* This same work was revised, expanded, and published in French at the end of his academic career—as a kind of capstone—as *Célébrer le Salut.*[17] Interestingly, this work is the co-publication of a Protestant and Catholic publishing house, embodying von Allmen's conviction that common prayer is the "irreplaceable and promising source of reconciled life together."[18]

The first section of this seminal work is primarily theological, articulating three key themes: worship as the celebration of salvation, worship as the manifestation of the church, and how worship, with its eschatological horizon, is both threat and promise for the world. The second section speaks more practically about the elements of worship, the participants in worship, the day and place of worship, etc. Bridel says that as a whole, the work "combines the precision of a manual with the freedom of an essay and the depth of a meditation."[19] Bridel goes on to describe the book as "calmly reformed, a polemic on one front against ritualism, and on the other front against the Enlightenment, while at the same time reminiscent of the deep ecumenical impulses seen in the WCC BEM and Lima documents."[20]

A key argument in this book (like Howard Hagemann's contemporaneous argument in *Pulpit and Table*) is the inseparability of the gospel proclaimed in worship in both word and sacrament. It was one of von Allmen's great satisfactions when the newly united Reformed Church in Switzerland declared the weekly celebration of the Eucharist normative for its congregations.[21]

In addition to this book on worship, von Allmen also wrote an important early volume on homiletics, *Preaching and Congregation,*[22] during the years when he was exercising this ministry weekly. In it, he often follows the theological lead of his friend Karl Barth, comparing the preacher to

16. von Allmen, "Jean-Jacques von Allmen, Liturgique-cours donné par le professeur."

17. von Allmen, *Célébrer le Salut.*

18. Bridel, "la passion de unite," 571.

19. Bridel, "la passion de unite," 571.

20. Bridel, "la passion de unite," 571.

21. Senn, "Worship, Doctrine, and Life," 454.

22. von Allmen, *Preaching & Congregation* (a translation of *La predication*).

the Virgin Mary, the bearer in words and flesh and human weakness of Divine glory. Tom Long calls von Allmen's work the "high water mark" of Reformed homiletics in the past century.[23]

The sacraments also received significant scholarly attention from von Allmen. His *Essai sur le repas du Seigneur* was written for the WCC Faith & Order Commission in 1966 and was immediately translated into English,[24] German, Italian, Japanese, and Spanish. It was recognized as one of the most generative pieces of ecumenical theology to emerge from that era.[25] In it, von Allmen's interpretive lens is primarily eschatological, and so he addresses various aspects of the sacrament in a dialectical way, echoing 'the already and the not yet.' For instance, von Allmen speaks of the Eucharist revealing the "limits" and the "fullness" of the church; he speaks of the meal as Communion with Christ and with others; he speaks of Christ's presence as both living bread and as sacrifice; and he underscores the importance of both anamnesis and epiclesis in the prayers surrounding the Supper.

His work on the sacrament of baptism was not published until later in his career. It is a combination of basic biblical and theological reflections on baptism, and contextual reflections in direct response to the challenge of a crumbling Christendom in Europe.[26] In it, one can see Barth's influence, as von Allmen stands, cross-armed and scowling at the widespread European practice of baptizing most infants. Though he does not question the *validity* of such baptisms, he writes that when done so, baptism loses its ecclesiastic dimension, its eschatological dimension, and its pneumatological character. It is, finally, "sociologically anachronistic and theologically irresponsible."[27]

This study will look much more carefully at these four major works on worship, preaching, and the sacraments in the next chapter. For now, note how they signal von Allmen's abiding interest in the reform of the church through the renewal of its worship.

His work in reform was not limited to his writing, however. With Wiebe Vos, a pastor of the Dutch Reformed church, von Allmen founded the *Societas Liturgica* in 1962, "an association for the promotion of ecumenical dialogue on worship, based on solid research, with the perspective

23. Day et al., *Reader on Preaching*, 11.

24. von Allmen, *Lord's Supper*.

25. Haquin, "Les sacrements de l'initiation chrétienne," 141.

26. von Allmen, *Pastorale du baptême*.

27. von Allmen, *Pastorale du baptême*.

of renewal and unity." This international and ecumenical community is just one example of the ecumenical dialogue and partnership that came to characterize so much of von Allmen's work—a theme to which we now turn.

THE ECUMENIST

Jean-Jacques von Allmen devoted himself tirelessly to ecumenical efforts in service of the church's unity. He had extensive knowledge of the academic and ecclesial realities of other countries and a deep appreciation for other traditions and his friends in them. This ecumenical work took two primary forms: writing and consulting.

Apart from the books we have already mentioned that have a significant ecumenical application (such as *The Lord's Supper*), von Allmen addressed ecumenical challenges head-on in a number of important works. One of them, *Le Saint Ministère,* interestingly, is his mid-career book on "ministry" as understood and articulated by the sixteenth century reformers. This book is a commentary on the twenty-eighth chapter of the Second Helvetic confession, but it develops themes pertinent to the ecumenical present: the diversity of ministries, apostolic succession, and the episcopate. Among his most startling conclusions is his belief that the absence of a diocesan bishop in the Reformed churches is more sociological than theological, owing, in von Allmen's view, to the indifference of the sixteenth century bishops to the reformers' complaints and calls to return to the gospel, which resulted in the "episcopalization" of the pastor. In order for reformed churches to be valid ecumenical partners, argues von Allmen, the Reformed protest against the Roman doctrine of the priesthood needs to be more clearly stated. Furthermore, a truly reformed doctrine of ministry needs to be articulated in a way that does not exclude a diversity of ministries, does not dismiss apostolic succession (understood as indissolubly doctrinal and pastoral), and that does claim episcopal dignity for all its pastors.

Another article that takes up ecumenical concerns is von Allmen's direct response to the problem of the recognition of the papacy by Protestants.[28] After a significant study of both history and the New Testament, von Allmen draws an ecumenically hopeful conclusion: "I believe that to the extent that he is the 'successor of Peter,' the Pope should become again simply the bishop of the Church of Peter and Paul. He thus might

28. von Allmen, "La primauté de l'Eglise de Pierre et du Paul."

become credible and acceptable to those who now reject how he justifies his ministry. In effect, this would signify that the Church of Rome, which has a vocational primacy, would renounce that primacy as a foundation for the ecclesiality of *other* local churches. It could become once again their simple and humble 'prima inter pares.'"[29]

In addition to his scholarship, von Allmen was an eager and valued participant in ecumenical discussions throughout his career. For example, in 1958, he presented a paper on "The Holy Spirit and Worship" in the European Section of the Liturgical Commission of Faith and Constitution.[30] And in 1960 he presented a paper to the ecumenical "Group of Dombes" on "Pastoral Authority according to the Reformed Confessions of Faith."

By the time of the meetings of Vatican II, von Allmen had considerable stature in the ecumenical movement and during one of the sessions was invited by Cardinal Bea to Rome. He remarked that the event of Vatican II gave renewed vigor to the ecumenical movement, making Protestants "ready to enter into dialogue, even in symphony, with the theology of Congar, of Küng, of Rahner."[31] Rhapsodically, he concludes: "Karl Barth has rendered for us the Creed and Vatican II [has rendered for us] the Church."[32]

But his largest ecumenical role was as a leader on the Faith & Order Commission of the World Council of Churches. At the fourth World Assembly, held in Uppsala (July 1968), von Allmen proposed a detailed analysis of the concept of secularization and theology of Christian worship. He actively participated in the final editing of the text whose title would simply be "Le Culte." Von Allmen also took part in the meetings at Louvain in August 1971 and Accra in 1974, at which the tripartite structure for BEM was drawn up. He is thus at the very center of ecumenical reflection that fed teachers of all nationalities and denominations.

In 1971 von Allmen took a partial leave from his responsibilities in Neuchâtel to help found the Ecumenical Theological Research Institute of

---

29. von Allmen, "La primauté de l'Eglise de Pierre et du Paul," 91. Interestingly, the recently installed Pope Francis may be heading in something like this direction, as he de-emphasizes many of his papal titles, preferring to be known as simply the "bishop of Rome."

30. This was almost certainly a reworking of his inaugural lecture at Neuchâtel.

31. von Allmen, "Une réforme dans l'Eglise," 55.

32. von Allmen, "Une réforme dans l'Eglise," 55. His interest in conciliar ecclesiology continued to develop, and he served as an advisor to the Swiss Catholic Synod in 1972.

Tantur near Jerusalem, where he served first as vice-president, and then president until 1974.

In recognition of his commitment to ecumenism, von Allmen received honorary doctorates from three universities: the Reformed University of Strasbourg, the Faculty of the University of Aberdeen, and the Orthodox Faculty of Cluj in Romania.

Jean-Jacques von Allmen retired from teaching in 1980, and after a long illness, he died in Neuchâtel on December 17, 1994.

SUMMARY

It is difficult to summarize a life or its influence on a generation of pastors and scholars. It is certainly true that von Allmen's thought has been taken seriously in the ecumenical world for half a century. Respect and recognition has also grown in his own reformed church tradition, especially in the last decade or so.[33] Yet the salient feature of von Allmen's liturgical theology is not so much its wide influence but rather the depth of his insight and the height of his vision for the church—insight and vision gleaned not through ivory-tower contemplation but by day-to-day ministry in local congregations. It is a mark of his piety and sanctification that von Allmen saw in his parochial sheep not just another flock with its own faults and foibles. Instead, he saw and experienced and testified to the sublime truth that those same people, animated by the Holy Spirit, are the very body of Christ. It is hard to say who have been more blessed by von Allmen's life and work: those who, at a distance, read and digest his works of theology, written at the intersection of worship and church, or the parishioners who received from his person the Word in proclamation and sacrament each week.

33. Bridel, "la passion de unite," 574.

Chapter 3

Persistent Themes

The Christian cult,[1] because it sums up the history of salvation, enables the church to become itself, to become conscious of itself and to confess what it essentially is.... To learn to know the Church and to understand its life, it is indispensable to go to church and to take part in its worship.

—Jean-Jacques von Allmen[2]

We turn now to Jean-Jacques von Allmen's writing in order to articulate his liturgical ecclesiology. We will be looking at von Allmen's ecclesiological reflections, embedded in his liturgical theology, to clarify and categorize his thoughts on the nature of the church. The next chapter will examine what von Allmen wrote about the church's characteristic Nicene marks—unity,

1. It is worth making a brief terminological remark concerning von Allmen's use of the French term *cult*. Many of his English-speaking editors and publishers simply leave the term un-translated, preferring the Romance overtones of the Latin *colere* to the Anglo-Saxon *weorthscipe*. The term refers to religious externals—the words and symbols and gestures that make up the church's rites. This stands in contrast to the way some others might define worship, and even in some contrast with Biblical words commonly translated "worship," but which mean other things, such as "giving worth" or "service." The use of the term *cult*, then, may signify "the care with which highly valued persons, places, or objects are ritually recognized and revered. By extension, *cultus* refers to an organized system of worship: all the ritual actions by which communities and individuals outwardly express their religious beliefs and so seek contact and communion with God." See Bradshaw, *New Dictionary of Liturgy and Worship*, 140.

2. von Allmen, *Worship*, 43.

holiness, catholicity, and apostolicity. But first, a brief introduction to three of von Allmen's key theological themes—themes that are at the heart of everything else he writes about, concerning worship, preaching, and the sacraments: worship as the recapitulation of salvation history, worship as the manifestation of the church,[3] and the church at worship as both threat and promise to the world.

WORSHIP AS THE RECAPITULATION OF SALVATION HISTORY

One of the central claims of von Allmen's liturgical ecclesiology, articulated throughout his works, is this: the cult is "the recapitulation of the history of salvation."[4] That is to say, the church's acts of worship sum up and confirm God's dealings with humanity throughout time—from the moment of creation through the final consummation of all things. Those dealings focus in particular on one unique historical fulcrum: the incarnation, ministry, death, resurrection, and ascension of Jesus of Nazareth.[5] Thus, worship is concerned about temporal past, present, and future as they are distilled and focused in Christ.

Worship

Jesus' own life is fundamentally liturgical, i.e., it is the worship acceptable to God. One of von Allmen's valuable contributions to the field of liturgical theology is his identification of and focus on two liturgical phases of Jesus' earthly ministry. Mirroring the shape of the synoptic gospels, the first

---

3. These ideas did not originate with von Allmen, and many after him articulate the same themes. See, for example, the gloss James K. A. Smith gives to the notion: "What we do in worship is both a rehearsal of the entire history of the world and a rehearsal for kingdom come" (Smith, *Imagining the Kingdom,* 2).

4. von Allmen, *Worship,* 21, 32. Note that von Allmen's use of the term *recapitulation* here may borrow from authors such as Irenaeus or Lancelot Andrewes, but von Allmen's use is neither about Christ's recapitulation of Adam's human life nor of the specifically Eucharistic recapitulation of Christ's sacrifice. It is instead a sense of the act of Christian worship as a recapitulation of the entire history of God's salvific work in the world. "Liturgy connects the Church with the history of salvation. . . . It unites the Church of all places and times around the permanently decisive *magnalia Dei*" (von Allmen, *Preaching & Congregation,* 36).

5. von Allmen, *Preaching & Congregation,* 33.

is a Galilean phase, encompassing Jesus' healing and teaching ministry in and around Galilee, on "the appeal addressed to [men], on the choice with which they are confronted."[6] The second is a Jerusalemite phase, centering around the events of Jesus' passion, his death on the cross, and then the "irruption of the eschatological resurrection," culminating in the ascension where "Jesus leaves his own, blessing them and sending them forth into the world to bear witness to himself." This phase "explains, justifies, and elicits the true content of the first."[7] These two phases of Jesus' ministry correlate to the primary phases of the church's liturgy—i.e., the mass of the catechumens and the mass of the faithful.[8] The worship of Christ then, while anchored in a particular time and place, is not bound by it, but rather has a scope beyond time—it "brings to concrete embodiment his whole work, which was prepared before the incarnation, has borne fruit since the ascension, and will be manifested in glory on the day of his appearing."[9]

Von Allmen argues that there are two senses in which the cult is then the recapitulation of salvation history: the chronological sense and the theological sense. Theologically, Christ's work reflects his three-fold office; that is, it has prophetic, priestly, and royal components. These correspond to the revelation of the divine will, the fulfillment of the divine will, and the safeguarding of that will (and thus, even these have a chronological component: past, present, and future). The cult "sums up all that God has taught us of his will . . . all that God has done to reconcile the world to himself . . . [and] all that God has made of those who accept reconciliation with himself."[10]

More than this, others note in von Allmen's emphasis on recapitulation a further theological focus—a "Trinitarian integrating impulse," which sees Christian worship as a "locus for divine action" and thus not "isolated from God's actions of creation and recreation, redemption and eschatological kingdom-building." Liturgical scholar Bryan Spinks writes that von Allmen explicitly assumes the unity of God's being and God's work, arguing that "the doctrine of the trinity is a confession of the unity

---

6. von Allmen, *Worship*, 23.

7. von Allmen, *Worship*, 23.

8. See von Allmen, *Preaching & Congregation*, 21, 23, 177–78.

9. von Allmen, *Worship*, 23.

10. von Allmen, *Worship*, 38.

and comprehensiveness of God's work, an invitation to approach liturgy in constant awareness of past, present, and future aspects of God's action."[11]

In a chronological sense, the church's worship, according to von Allmen, has three functions: anamnetic, proleptic, and affirmative. It is anamnetic: a sign of the past in the richest sense—not merely an exercise of memory but rather a "restoration of the past so that it becomes present and a promise." It is also proleptic, directed to the future, an "anticipation of [Christ's] return and a foreshadowing of the Kingdom." Finally, it is not only past and future oriented, it affirms and glorifies a "Messianic present," in which the "earth is lifted toward heaven."[12]

Further, von Allmen contends that when the church gathers to pray, it is actually advancing the history of the world's salvation, because God hears it. "Every true Christian prayer is the bearer and agent of history, it brings the end of the world closer. . . . When the Church gathers for prayer, the church is the instrument of God's purpose for the world."[13] In fact, for von Allmen, one of the three fundamental purposes of common prayer is simply the retelling and celebration of the "mighty acts of God."[14]

Since the work of salvation is completed in Christ, how can we say that its history continues into the present day? The answer lies in the work of the Holy Spirit, by whom humans are "launched on the full flood tide of salvation," "grafted onto the cardinal event of Good Friday and Easter." By the power of the Spirit, in the anamnesis of the church, Christ's work becomes the "ontological reality of those who rejoice in it and live by it." And since the church is the "privileged sphere where this actualization takes place," her worship is thus "one of the most conspicuous agents in the process of saving history."[15]

Beyond the two-fold heart of Lord's Day worship, von Allmen does not say much about how his understanding of worship's relationship to time (salvation history in past, present and future) should inform the structure of worship itself, i.e., the order in which elements of worship should be celebrated. He does say that some structure is important, rooted in the doctrine of the incarnation.[16] And he does distinguish and call for a balance

---

11. Spinks, "Place of Christ in Liturgical Prayer," 289–93.

12. von Allmen, *Worship*, 34–35.

13. von Allmen, "Theological Meaning of Common Prayer," 127–28.

14. von Allmen, "Theological Meaning of Common Prayer," 129.

15. von Allmen, *Worship*, 40.

16. von Allmen, *Worship*, 80, 288.

between the objective (sacramental) and subjective (sacrificial) elements in worship, acknowledging that no element is purely one or the other.[17] When he explicitly addresses the order in time in which the elements are to be celebrated, though, he avoids pronouncing blessing on a particular order. Some orders are "more intelligent" and others are "more fervent"—but they are all legitimate so far as they "respect the constituent features . . . of the cult."[18]

Those features center on word and sacrament, the Galilean and Jerusalemite phases of the service. Thus, von Allmen joins his voice with many other liturgical reformers in the 1960s, calling for a return to the ancient biblical pattern of apostolic witness and weekly Communion in the body and blood of Christ, the "pulse-beat of liturgical life."[19]

Preaching

The same theme of worship as recapitulation echoes through von Allmen's treatment of preaching. A few examples will suffice. At the very outset of *Preaching and Congregation*, he writes of the "miracle" of preaching, which is that it is not merely speech *about* God, but speech *by* God. Jean-Jacques von Allmen frames this as an expression of the outworking of salvation history: "Our preaching continues the past preaching of Jesus, and looks forward to the Word he will speak at his return. That is why God himself is at work, in this present day, when we preach."[20] He elaborates on this later, marshaling the Johannine insight that "Christ is the very Word of God" to support his contention that "the Word which God speaks to the world is for us a Word which has already been pronounced; for even the Word which he will pronounce at the last Judgment will not bring anything essentially new; it will only make manifest and concrete for every man what He has said in his Son."[21]

In another place, speaking about the duty of the preacher to translate and make present the Word of God for a particular people in a particular place and time, von Allmen argues for the narrative *content* of the gospel, that God's grace toward God's people is encountered in a story—a salvation

17. von Allmen, *Worship*, 181.

18. von Allmen, *Worship*, 288.

19 von Allmen, *Worship*, 284.

20. von Allmen, *Preaching & Congregation*, 7.

21. von Allmen, *Preaching & Congregation*, 22.

history: "In preaching the Gospel, we enroll our parishioners in a story; we do not explain an idea to them."[22]

Finally, von Allmen compares the tension between sermon and liturgy to the eschatological tension experienced between the ascension and the second coming, the already and the not yet. He writes:

> If the liturgy attaches the Church to the history of salvation, the sermon recalls to her that she participates in that history in the midst of this world. Two escapist paths are thus barred: escape toward a Church complacently practicing a docetic liturgiolatry, sheltered from the world by her form of worship, and escape towards a Church indulging in breathless prophetic activity, cut off from the peace of God, from her eschatological rest by continuous homiletical exertion.[23]

Sacraments

In a similar way, von Allmen's writing on the sacraments returns persistently to the theme of recapitulation. His treatment of the Lord's Supper begins with an exploration of anamnesis and epiclesis. Anamnesis, he argues, is more than just an act of memory, a rehearsal of Jesus' suffering, death, and resurrection. In the Lord's Supper, the church participates in God's saving action in history: "Through this celebration they claim the benefits of what Christ did once for all, they take their place therein, and the history of salvation, of which they are commemorating the crowning moment, becomes the history of their own salvation."[24] The past-into-the-present dynamic of anamnesis is balanced by the present-into-the-future dynamic of the epiclesis, which ensures that the church remains a praying church rather than a triumphant one, a church simultaneously pleading that God's kingdom may come and experiencing that coming in a rich way. Even the Great Prayer of Thanksgiving, following the pattern of Acts 4:24–30, sets out a preface that "reminds God of what he has done to create and save the world, and an act of intercession that the history of salvation might be continued, that the church should be integrated into this history and that she might participate in its completion."[25]

22. von Allmen, *Preaching & Congregation*, 21.
23. von Allmen, *Preaching & Congregation*, 36.
24. von Allmen, *Lord's Supper*, 27.
25. von Allmen, *Lord's Supper*, 102.

God's saving action in history, commemorated and expected in the supper, stretches not only backwards and forwards in time but also reaches wide to encircle the whole church: "At the moment when the Church meets in Eucharistic worship, the total Christ, head and body is present: the Christ who came, who reigns and who is coming, and in Him, because of Him, with Him, the whole communion of saints, in whom the history of salvation is accomplished."[26]

In a similar way, the sacrament of baptism unites the baptized both to Christ and to the body of Christ—that is, the church, the "messianic people of the last days."[27] For von Allmen, baptism is a sort of personal anticipation of the last judgment. It situates itself in the ambiance of the great eschatological agony, then proclaiming and making real Christ's ultimate victory.[28] Baptism associates the baptized both with Christ's death and his resurrection, and it anticipates or marks a first step in a new life.

In his primary work on baptism, *Pastorale du Baptême*, von Allmen contends that the events between Good Friday and Easter provide the culminating and decisive moments in God's salvation history. In them, God focused his *last* judgment of humanity and the world. Yet it is a judgment of love, because in it, Jesus became a substitute for humanity.

Baptism links the person who receives it to the major event in the history of salvation: through baptism, one dies with Christ, is buried with Christ, and is raised with Christ—it gives life to those who believe in him and have left death behind. Baptism, therefore, creates a break in the unfolding of the baptized life. It radically shifts from a before to an after, just as Christ's coming and death radically shift all history from a before to an after.[29]

WORSHIP AS MANIFESTATION OF THE CHURCH

The second key theme coloring von Allmen's liturgical ecclesiology is worship as the manifestation of the church. When God's people are gathered to worship—when the church is at church—it learns what and who and whose it is: "by its worship, the Church becomes itself, becomes conscious

26. von Allmen, *Lord's Supper*, 47.

27. von Allmen, *Pastorale du Baptême*, II.2.a.

28. von Allmen, *Pastorale du Baptême*, II.2.b.

29. von Allmen, *Pastorale du Baptême*, II.2.d.

of itself, and confesses itself as a distinctive entity."[30] This is not an idea that originates with von Allmen, nor is he the only liturgical theologian who embraces it. The father of liturgical theology, Alexander Schmemann, wrote that it is within the liturgy that "the church is informed of her cosmical and eschatological vocation, receives the power to fulfill it, and thus truly becomes what she is—the sacrament, in Christ, of the kingdom."[31] Likewise, the recovery of the ecclesiological doctrine of the Mystical Body of Christ in the nineteenth century came to fruition at Vatican II, where one of its key documents, *Sancrosanctum Concillium,* maintains that "the Church reveals herself most clearly when a full complement of God's holy people, united in prayer and in a common liturgical service, especially the Eucharist, exercise a thorough and active participation."[32] And Peter Brunner, a key source for von Allmen, writes, "Church worship, as an assembly in the name of Jesus, of the Christian community, is what might be described as the true manifestation of the church on earth. The occurrence of such a meeting is the epiphany of the Church."[33]

For von Allmen, however, the notion of the church being most 'itself' at worship is closely linked to the idea just discussed, worship as the recapitulation of salvation history. This is because the church is not fundamentally an institution or organism. It is fundamentally a *liturgical* assembly, emerging out of and living into a story. For von Allmen, there is an inevitably *narrative* character to all Christian liturgy and hence all Christian liturgical assemblies.

The term used to name the church in the New Testament—*ecclesia*—is used, von Allmen notes, less for etymological reasons than because it is the LXX translation of *qâhâl Yahwé,* the assembly of the people of God, the recipients of God's action in history: saved from Egypt and confirmed in covenant worship at Mount Sinai. The solemn assemblies recorded at various points in scripture (Deut 9, 18; Josh 8; 1 Kgs 8; 2 Chr 20; 2 Chr 29–30; 2 Kgs 23; Neh 8–9, etc.) are marked by the same things that mark the present assemblies of the church: divine initiative, divine presence,

---

30. von Allmen, *Worship,* 42.

31. Schmemann, "Liturgy and Theology," 92.

32. Second Vatican Council, *"Sacrosanctum Concilium."* The fact that this section focuses on the importance of the bishop only strengthens the point when one recalls how Roman Catholic polity locates ecclesiality in the episcopate—in the person of the bishop.

33. Brunner quoted in von Allmen, *Worship,* 42.

the proclamation of the divine Word, and the sealing of the encounter by sacrifices.[34] When the church gathers, it rehearses the saving acts of God in the past, re-members the Body of Christ, and anticipates and lives into her eschatological end. At worship, the church is "supremely itself, visibly becoming what it mysteriously is: God's people gathered before him."[35]

To learn of the church, one may study dogmatic texts and confessions of faith, church history, personal piety and books of church order. But at worship, says von Allmen, the "fact of the church first emerges. . . . It is there it gives proof of itself, there where it is focused, and where we are led when we truly seek it, and it is from that point that it goes out into the world to exercise its mission."[36] If this is the case, then the church's true being is not revealed so much in its structure, or its catechesis, or its diaconate. These are not unimportant for von Allmen, but they take their cues from the church at worship, not the other way around.[37]

Connected to this point is von Allmen's claim about reform of the church. If indeed the "true character of the Church is revealed in and through its worship," then when the church is in need of reform, it is its worship that must be reformed.[38] Historically, the renewal of the church has always been marked by *liturgical* renewal. The great reforms of Israel, he notes, are liturgical reforms (cf. 2 Chr 29–30; 2 Kgs 23). The transition from old covenant to new covenant is a *liturgical* one; the day and place of worship change, the sacraments change.[39] Thus, for churches today hoping for renewal through improved vision statements, increased programming, youth-focused initiatives, or a type of "re-branding," von Allmen cautions:

> It is not a better catechesis, nor a reorganization of the Church, nor a new awareness of the appeal sounded in our ears by the weary and the heavy-laden—it is not these things which will justify the Church of our time: it is a liturgical reform because it is this which will justify in its repercussions this catechesis, this reorganization, this diaconate inasmuch as it will prevent them from degenerating

34. von Allmen, *Worship*, 43.

35. von Allmen, "Theological Meaning of Common Prayer," 126.

36. von Allmen, *Worship*, 42.

37. von Allmen, *Worship*, 53.

38. von Allmen is careful to be clear: it is not *by* its worship that the church is re-formed, but *in* it. It is the living and active Word of God that reforms the church. But it does so through a transformation of its worship, which then ripples out into the life of the church in all areas of its ministry. See von Allmen, *Worship*, 54.

39. von Allmen, *Worship*, 44.

into a Biblicist intellectualism, an Erastian legalism, or a socialistic activism.[40]

Preaching

Worship as a whole manifests the fundamental identity of the church. Key elements of the worship service do as well. Preaching, for example, says von Allmen, both *gathers* in the church and *builds up* the church. These are distinct functions of the Word of God. Missionary preaching is the announcement of the Gospel, the *kerygma*, which, "gathers together in all nations and in all ages that eschatological people which is the Church,"[41] But because the "threat of dispersion" is always present until Christ returns, the church engages in "common liturgical preaching," preaching that reproves and exhorts, that encourages growth in faith, that "watches over the assembly, to safeguard it and to give it its full meaning"[42]—in short, preaching that nourishes and builds up the church.[43] The first type of preaching points to and naturally leads to conversion and its sacrament, baptism. The second type moves toward the place where the church finds itself fed by Christ: the Eucharistic table.[44]

Linking the theme of manifestation with the theme of recapitulation, von Allmen argues that when the church gathers, it knows and becomes itself. It does so not by looking at some purified and perfected hoped-for

40. von Allmen, *Worship*, 54. See also von Allmen, "Theological Frame."

41. von Allmen, *Preaching & Congregation*, 9.

42. von Allmen, *Preaching & Congregation*, 11.

43. Preaching is not the *only* means by which the church is built up. Jean-Jacques von Allmen specifically mentions a handful of others, including the diaconate, the witness of members, catechism, Bible study, discipline, and the regular liturgy. See von Allmen, *Preaching & Congregation*, 10.

44. Interestingly, von Allmen complains in this section of *Preaching & Congregation* that too much of the proclamation in his area churches is of the first sort here when it ought rather to be the second sort: "In our Church . . . we are in great danger of preaching as though baptism still lay, and always would lie, ahead of us, as if we were condemned to pace the Egyptian shore of the Red Sea, as if God had not translated us out of the power of dryness into the kingdom of the Son of His love. . . . Our sermons do not draw our congregation along in the movement of the history of salvation; a movement which advances, which allows continuous growth. . . . It would be an insult to the grace of baptism to admit the Baptist position by calling in question, through continual missionary appeal, the fact that our members have already entered into the body of Christ" (von Allmen, *Preaching & Congregation*, 10–11).

version of itself, a dieter looking at a photo-shopped image of himself as motivation for self-improvement. No, the church looks at Jesus Christ and learns from him "what sort of Bride it is that he loves. It is on Christ's face that the Church learns who it is."[45] Thus, the church finds its life and identity in Christ's identity—specifically, the three-fold office of Christ. It is embodied in the church's liturgical life: a Galilean or prophetic phase, with the sermon at its center; a Jerusalemite or priestly phase, with the Eucharist at its heart, while the third office, the royal office, has its reflection, according to von Allmen, in the "practice of Christian obedience throughout the week which the Sunday service initiates."[46]

Sacraments

In a similar way, the church's sacramental celebrations define who she is in relation to the world, to the other churches, and to God. In fact, von Allmen identifies a handful of descriptive adjectives to describe the church's fundamental identity, and primary among those adjectives are "baptismal" and "Eucharistic."

In baptism one is joined to the church in the presence of the community to which new members are admitted. Here especially, the church learns its identity, as the covenant community celebrates the salvation offered in Christ. Of course, baptism has a multitude of meanings, but among the central ones are both unity with Christ in his own death and resurrection (cf. Rom 6) as well as unity and membership in the church, the body of Christ. Baptism is thus the gateway through which new Christians are given the rights and duties associated with membership in the church. Among these, according to von Allmen, are the right and duty to bear witness to the Gospel, to live ethically, and to "lead a life worthy of the calling to which you have been called."[47]

In addition, members in the church—those who have been baptized—have the right and duty to sit at the Lord's Table and partake in the eschatological meal. The Eucharist "restores and confirms those who communicate and enables them to grow in their baptismal resurrection, it reveals the

---

45. von Allmen, "Theological Frame," 12.

46. von Allmen, *Preaching & Congregation*, 43.

47. von Allmen, *Pastorale du Baptême*, II.1.c.

Church as a community of those who know what succeeds the world and its history and who already live by it."[48]

And though baptism is important for understanding what the church is, von Allmen is strongest when speaking of the Lord's Supper as the determinative moment in worship where the church realizes its identity. The church's "foundation" and "fulfillment" are found in the supper.[49] He goes so far as to argue that there need be nothing said in worship beyond that which is enacted in the supper. And further: "The same applies to the church's mission in the world: the church has nothing to say other than what can find its inspiration or confirmation in the Supper."[50]

The structure of the church is also revealed in the supper, according to von Allmen. In fact the "elements of ecclesiastical structure and organization which normally have no Eucharistic function or reference are unrelated to the essential nature of the Church and therefore irrelevant for ecclesiology, if not suspect."[51] Boiled down to its most simple and coherent structure, the church is comprised of two poles: a shepherd and a flock, a witness of Christ and the members of his body. These exist in a reciprocal relationship, as both are required for the existence of the other.

Likewise, von Allmen speaks of a two-fold mystery of the church that is revealed when it gathers to celebrate the Lord's Supper. This mystery is that the church is both a sign of the presence of the Kingdom of God in the world, and a sign of the presence of the world before God. In each local congregation, the kingdom of God is seen when it gathers at table, for there the congregation is identified as a "messianic people celebrating the history of salvation and therefore integrated into this history by its very Eucharistic celebration."[52] The church is doubly sacramental, then, representing also the world before God—and representing not only believers, but things (bread, wine), time, and space. "At the moment of the Eucharist, creation finds access again to real worship, and recovers her primary orientation, which is doxological."[53] In another section he continues:

> That is the truth about the Church and her duty: to hold fast in this
> tension between what she already has and what she still awaits,

48. von Allmen, *Lord's Supper*, 37.

49. von Allmen, *Lord's Supper*, 19.

50. von Allmen, *Lord's Supper*, 27.

51. von Allmen, *Lord's Supper*, 44.

52. von Allmen, *Lord's Supper*, 47.

53. von Allmen, *Lord's Supper*, 49.

between what she already is and what she must become, between the fulfillment and the repetition of her prayer, between the Supper as messianic meal and the Supper as mere ambiguous prefiguration of that meal—without being made proud or idle by what she already has, or grieving or being discouraged as if she had nothing. By her Eucharistic prayer, she still calls in the name of the whole world for the coming of God's Kingdom; in the Eucharistic fulfillment she experiences already, on behalf of the whole world, the truth and reality of that kingdom.[54]

WORSHIP AND THE WORLD

One of von Allmen's favorite images of the church at worship is that of a beating heart. It is an image that does a number of things. First, it extends or amplifies a number of biblical images for the church in meaningful and suggestive ways. Second, it responds to a possible objection raised to von Allmen's focus on the church at worship as definitive of its ecclesial character. Finally, it points to a third preliminary theme: the church as both menace and promise for the world.

In a section in *Worship: Its Theology and Practice*, where von Allmen makes the turn from the church at worship to all the other ministries of the church, he writes that worship is the *heart* of the Christian community:

> The life of the Church pulsates like the heart by systole and diastole. As the heart is for the animal body, so the cult is for church life a pump which sends into circulation and draws it in again, it claims and it sanctifies. It is from the life of worship . . . that the Church spreads itself abroad into the world to mingle with it like leaven in the dough, to give it savour like salt, to irradiate it like light, and it is toward the cult—toward the Eucharist—that the Church returns from the world, like a fisherman gathering up his nets or a farmer harvesting his grain.[55]

To those who would protest that the church *is* much more, and *does* much more than we see in worship, von Allmen responds that all that is important about what the church is can be seen in worship. All that is significant about what it does can be seen in a distilled form or heard in echoes when the assembly of the baptized gathered to hear the Word of God proclaimed and

54. von Allmen, *Lord's Supper*, 106.
55. von Allmen, *Worship*, 55–56.

to offer the Eucharist in thanksgiving to God.. Church teaching that doesn't produce more faithful worshippers, acts of mercy that do not emerge from the church's life of prayer, church activities of any sort that are "indifferent" to being rooted in worship—all of these are faulty, profane, parasitic.

Threat and Promise[56]

If the church at worship retells salvation history, thereby learning, at worship, who it is, this means that the church finds itself *in relation to the world* as both threat[57] and promise. As worship is offered in the world, on behalf of the world, by the church, it underscores "the impermanence of the life of the world" in the scope of God's divine plan, while at the same time offering itself as a sign of eschatological hope, a transformation and a real future.[58]

For von Allmen, the distinction between world and church, sacred and profane, is an important one. He acknowledges that there are those, especially in the modern era, who think this distinction anachronistic. But von Allmen argues that eliminating the distinction is actually denying the incarnation, because to do so implies that "the world to come is too unreal or too remote to arouse here anything but wistful desire, or to bring into being any signs of its actual presence here below."[59] Distrust of this distinction, says von Allmen, emerges either from a kind of docetism, or an uncomfortableness with the eschatological tension of the already-but-not-yet nature of the world's redemption.[60]

Part of holding on to this tension, for von Allmen, is the church recognizing and claiming its "otherness," its sacred nature, while not shutting itself away from the world. No, argues von Allmen, though there has been an uncomfortably "close agreement" between the sacred and profane

56. Like the others, this theme runs throughout von Allmen's writing, and in addition to the sections cited below, it is especially prominent in the first chapter of his *Prophétisme sacramentel,* 9–53.

57. Fletcher Fleet, the translator, translates the French *menace* here as "threat" and sometimes as "menace." Both are apt.

58. von Allmen, *Worship,* 57.

59. von Allmen, *Worship,* 59.

60. Interestingly, von Allmen argues strongly that the profanation of the church—and the church's willing consent to that profanation—is seen quite clearly and painfully in what he calls the "degradation of the miracle of baptism" in which the sacrament becomes merely a "generalized folklore ceremony" taken for granted by all in a given society. See *Worship,* 59.

during the era of Christendom, the church in a new post-Christian era will benefit by regaining a clearer sense of its role in the world as a prophetic, priestly, and royal people. A new awareness of itself as a minority group in the world is being demonstrated, he argues, by both a liturgical and missionary renaissance.[61]

The worshipping church is to the world both a threat and a promise. It is a threat because it is a challenge to human righteousness, a foretaste of the last judgment, and a protest against worship aimed at anything other than the living God. Whenever the church assembles to worship, it renounces the world and the world's claim to offer human beings a "valid justification for their existence."[62] So, for example, the doxological declarations of the church are an anti-pagan polemic with a political overtone: when worshippers sing, "Praise *God* from whom all blessings flow," when they declare "*Thine* is the kingdom and the power and the glory," they reject all pretensions to these things that might be implicitly claimed by other forces—such as the seductive cultural narratives of consumerism, or explicitly claimed by the state and its demands of obedience.[63] This rejection is a proleptic judgment that prefigures the ultimate accounting of the church and the world at the "eschatological discrimination." Christian worship "unites those who, by anticipation, have sacramentally undergone the process of the Last Judgment by the very fact of their baptism, by becoming associated with that determinative foreshadowing of the Last Judgment which was the death and resurrection of Christ."[64] Christian worship makes plain this threat, this challenge, not only in its doxologies, but in its prayers, its preaching, and in the Eucharist. In its prayers, it petitions "Thy kingdom come," which not only expresses hope but also asks the judge to come and for the world to be judged.[65] The threat is evident in preaching insofar as preaching calls upon people to make a decision of eschatological import—to "entrust their life to the One alone who can deliver them from perdition."[66] And the threat is also evident at the Lord's Supper where, though the 'medicine of salvation' is offered, the threshold contains a warning for those who are not

---

61. von Allmen, *Worship*, 61.
62. von Allmen, *Worship*, 63.
63. von Allmen, *Worship*, 63.
64. von Allmen, *Worship*, 64.
65. von Allmen, *Worship*, 66.
66. von Allmen, *Worship*, 65.

believers and who might eat and drink to their condemnation.[67] Finally, the very structure of worship, according to von Allmen, anticipates the last judgment because it includes these two moments, the first of which calls for a decision and the second "where the faithful are welcomed to the joy of the Messianic feast."[68]

The worship of the church is not just menace or threat. It is also a promise to the world because of Jesus Christ, the one "in whom the world, if it consents to renounce itself . . . regains its true destiny."[69] By its worship, the church serves in a vicarious and priestly capacity, representing and leading the entire universe in the worship that it was originally intended to offer. God's intention in creation, maintains von Allmen, was a liturgical one.[70] Hence, at worship, the church shows the world "the past it ought never to have lost and the future promised to it."[71] A lover of creatures,[72] von Allmen argues that the church's ministry is not just representative of people but also the whole of creation, so that its sighs and groans may be "transformed into singing."[73] He explicitly rejects the idea that nature is the world's true priest and that humans must join its song. No, it is the other way around: nature seeks to join in the worship offered by the church. In fact, says von Allmen, the baptismal power of the church's worship means that it not only takes up the chirping of birds and the whale-song, but in Christ and his death and resurrection, it has the power to pardon and fulfill

67. Jean-Jacques von Allmen notes that the formula for the liturgical dismissal prior to the Mass of the Faithful has transmogrified from an anathema to a benediction, yet the "very fact that there has been maintained (in the East, up to the present day) an exclusion of the non-baptized and the excommunicate at the moment when the Eucharistic celebration was about to begin, is a sign that the cult forms a prelude to the Last Judgment" (von Allmen, *Worship*, 67).

68. von Allmen, *Worship*, 66.

69. von Allmen, *Worship*, 68.

70. von Allmen, *Worship*, 69.

71. von Allmen, *Worship*, 70.

72. According to multiple sources, von Allmen was especially fond of visiting zoos. See Montmollin, "Jean-Jacques von Allmen" and also Old, "Reminiscences and Reflections."

73. von Allmen, *Worship*, 73. Particularly interesting here is von Allmen's argument for the cultural contextualization of worship: "To refuse to open the doors of the Christian cult to the world is not to love the world, not to pity it; it is to despise it based on a Marcionite dualism, to doubt the sanctifying power of the Word of God and of prayer, the possibility of transforming all creation into a song of thanksgiving (1 Tim 4:4) if we forbid the forms, the colours, the accents, the rhythms of the world to have any contact with the sphere of Christian worship."

all non-Christian or pagan worship, so that all in such worship—its purpose, its appeal, its use of the materials of the world—might be cleansed, reborn, redirected, and restored.[74]

Evangelization

Aware of the collapse of Christendom and the church's increased missionary situation in the world today, von Allmen asks (rhetorically) whether such a situation requires the church to abandon liturgical forms so that it may "appeal to the world with more forceful directness." The question itself, maintains von Allmen, betrays a "deep misunderstanding as to the aim and purpose" of worship.[75] It is not primarily aimed at the world, but at God. Recall the image of the heart with which this section began. The church is oriented toward God in the systole, toward the world in the diastole. There cannot be one without the other, nor can the two be conflated. Yes, von Allmen says, the church should put more energy into its evangelistic efforts, and it can always serve God in the world with more vigor and obedience. But one should not confuse these valuable things with the worship the church offers as the assembly of the baptized, "those whom the Gospel has reached, converting them, turning them to God and gathering them into the Church whence they will be able both to confront the world and encounter God."[76]

At the same time, von Allmen recognizes that church worship does indeed have an evangelistic aspect, especially in its first movement, the mass of the catechumens (or those preparing for baptism). He appreciatively quotes Karl Barth, who says that while worship has its pragmatic (i.e., evangelistic) uses, it cannot be justified on that account. Indeed, while evangelism is not

74. von Allmen, *Worship*, 76–77. Jean-Jacques von Allmen does not say much about *how* this pardon and fulfillment actually happens, though he does speak of it in strangely political terms. He notes that there are times when a "nation welcomes the Gospel and begins to respond to it by conversation and self-consecration," and its own national distinctiveness is added to the church, thereby contributing to diversity in the church's dogmatic structures, ecclesiastical systems, and liturgies. See von Allmen, *Worship*, 74–75.

75. von Allmen, *Worship*, 77.

76. von Allmen, *Worship*, 78. According to von Allmen, worship that is "public" in the full sense of the word (meaning available for any and all to witness and participate in) is a type of "perversion." Worship, he maintains, is for those who believe; communion is for the baptized. Yet he also distinguishes between preaching and worship and declares that the former does wish to be—indeed, needs to be—public. See von Allmen, *Worship*, 61–62.

only a concern for the non-baptized but also for the baptized—who must constantly struggle against the world—it is not the *primary* concern: "If living in the Christian period has made us largely forget the duty of evangelization, or if it has located evangelization chiefly in the cult, the end of the Christian period must not lead us into the opposite error of forgetting the necessity of the cult for its own sake."[77] In fact, von Allmen declares that by the mere fact of its celebration, worship has an evangelizing force because it is a "power radiating joy, peace, freedom, order, and love."

At such a statement, one may wonder what sort of worship was offered in the parish churches in Neuchâtel, Lucerne, and Lignières, and whether those churches—with all that radiating joy, peace, freedom, order and love—resemble much the churches of 21st century North America. There are times, of course, when the church's life expressed in its worship does indeed pulsate with divine power. And this is one of the most remarkable things about von Allmen's writing: that all his extraordinary, far-reaching, theological insight emerges from someone deeply engaged in the very ordinary and everyday work of a pastor among garden-variety Christians, teaching and visiting, baptizing and marrying and burying, preparing worship, and preaching and presiding at the table each Lord's Day.

77. von Allmen, *Worship*, 79.

CHAPTER 4

Ecclesial Identity

THE HEART OF THIS project follows: a survey of Jean-Jacques von Allmen's central books on worship, preaching, and the sacraments, looking at his liturgical theology through our ecclesiological lens. We begin with a preliminary survey of descriptive adjectives—both descriptive and aspirational—that von Allmen used in a number of different places to describe the church. These adjectives supplement the four at the center of our work. The study then proceeds to a closer examination of the four Nicene marks of ecclesial identity, concluding with an examination of the church's activities.

MARKS AND ADJECTIVES

Von Allmen's farewell lecture to the University of Neuchâtel was entitled "Les marques de l'Église"—the Marks of the Church. It is not fundamentally a work of liturgical theology but rather a survey of the New Testament data about the church's identity. In it von Allmen names eight "marks" which the New Testament churches all had in common. First among them is apostolic. "A church," he writes, "is a local Christian congregation founded by an apostle or his claim settled within the church by an apostle."[1] Second, any Christian congregation recognizes the books of the Hebrew Bible as Holy Scripture. Third—the most crucial, if the most obvious, according to von Allmen—is that a church must confess the Christian faith. By this von Allmen does not mean adherence to an ideology or morality, but participation

1. von Allmen, "Les Marques De L'Église," 98.

60

in a history. Alongside this is the embrace of the normative testimony of the eyewitnesses to Jesus' resurrection—the gospels and other books in the New Testament, which serve as the standard of faith and life. Fourth, the church is a community to which believers have access through baptism. Fifth, the church meets on the first day of the week to celebrate, in a meal, the death and resurrection of Jesus. Sixth, a Christian congregation prays eschatologically for the coming of the reign of God it has already tasted. This includes, in particular, the regular use of the Lord's Prayer. Seventh, a church is aware of a specific task it has to perform in the world: to bear witness to the salvation granted and lived in Christ. This witness takes the shape of loving one another according to Jesus' command in the gospel of John. Christian ethics emerges from eschatological vocation. Finally, a church is localized in a particular time and place. Von Allmen concludes by suggesting that such a list "offers to churches a mirror of what they would be if they were faithful. It therefore provides an outline of the reform that constantly awaits any church."[2]

In addition to this list of identifying marks, von Allmen also makes use of lists of descriptive adjectives in a number of places in his writing about worship and the sacraments.[3] These words function as liturgical (rather than strictly theological) keys to the church's self-understanding. Two of them—Apostolic and Catholic—can be considered in their appropriate place below, alongside their Nicene neighbors. The other adjectives, supplementing that list, are summarized briefly here.

Eschatological. There is much in the church's worship that is deemed "eschatological" by von Allmen. Prayers are eschatological, the Lord's Supper is eschatological, and the church's symbols are, above all, eschatological.[4] But the church itself is eschatological in that its "own true life is situated beyond the present world."[5] It is called to transcend the world, to renounce the world. One of the practical implications of this insight, for von Allmen, is the clear distinction drawn between church and world. The church is composed, says von Allmen, "for the purpose of worship, of baptized persons who are aware of their baptism and eager not to belie it . . .

---

2. von Allmen. "Les Marques De L'Église," 97–107.

3. These lists are found in key sections in *Worship*, as well as in "Theological Frame."

4. von Allmen, *Worship*, 99.

5. von Allmen, "Theological Frame," 12.

so a liturgical renewal will have as a necessary corollary a fresh awareness of baptism."[6]

Diaconal. The church, following the example of Christ, learns in worship that it is a servant community, sent to minister to others. For von Allmen, this means two things. First, that it exists not for itself, but for the world. It is to learn at worship to have the "attitude of a servant who is attentive to the true needs of the world and not only willing but able to help bring help to those needs."[7] Second, the church is a "living body whose members are diversified in their functions and importance."[8]

Local. Von Allmen calls the local church the "epiphany *hic et nunc* of the Holy Church of God." The catholicity of the church, he says, does not uproot it from its local soil. It has the right and obligation to love the very diverse places where it is planted and welcome those places into worship. Through baptism, the church's local identity is not washed away, but purified and enhanced. This will mean, says von Allmen, that there will always be some tension between local expression and tradition. But if there is to be liturgical renewal, "indigenous language, music, art, and rhythm must be allowed their place in the local Church."

Nuptial. One of von Allmen's favorite adjectives centers on the biblical image of the church as the bride of Christ.[9] In worship, then, the church learns that it is a nuptial community. He prefers this term in some ways to "Eucharistic" because the latter is so all encompassing. But the bride of Christ has said "yes" to the divine appeal. Jesus and the church have promised themselves to one another. Further, the bride now waits expectantly for Christ's second coming, and "lives in the strength of that promise."[10] It is a community of hope. It is also a community of love.

Eucharistic. By "Eucharistic," von Allmen means that the church finds itself at worship to be a community that orients itself toward God in its memorial and thanksgiving, but also to turn toward the world in a priestly posture, taking on, "if only by means of intercession, the anthropological,

6. von Allmen, "Theological Frame," 12.

7. von Allmen, "Theological Frame," 13.

8. von Allmen, *Worship*, 50.

9. It may be that von Allmen's fondness for this image comes in part from what was by all accounts a very happy marriage.

10. von Allmen, *Worship*, 47.

historical, and cosmic dimensions comprehended by the death of Jesus Christ."[11]

Baptismal. For von Allmen, the church's baptismal identity is closely tied to its holiness in this respect: the church is not the world, it is marked off as a separate people. It embraces the world, but the world is only present in worship insofar as it, too, has been baptized, died to itself and to sin in order to discover its true identity.

NICENE NOTES/MARKS OF THE CHURCH

The Nicene-Constantinopolitan Creed[12] uses four adjectives to describe the church: One, Holy, Catholic, and Apostolic. In Latin, the phrase is *et unam, sanctum, catholicam et apostolicam ecclesiam.* In his classic work, *Models of the Church,* Avery Cardinal Dulles notes the distinction between "church" in the sociological, descriptive sense—i.e., any group that calls itself church, any group to which a person might belong—and the more abstract theological notion of "capital-C" Church as the "mystery of Christ as the community of those who believe in him and are assembled in his name."[13] He further notes, "Since the first century, efforts have been made in every generation to establish criteria" by which one might discern whether churches of the descriptive sociological sort are indeed churches of the theological sort—part of the "true Church."[14] The Nicene marks were precisely those sorts of criteria, used early on by Irenaeus, Tertullian, and Augustine.[15] These marks became especially important to theologians doing polemical ecclesiology in the years following the Protestant Reformation, when there was increased urgency to define and defend what the church was. Today, Dulles says, we commonly use these four adjectives as theological "norms"—descriptively, of the true church, and prescriptively, as aspirational goals for the visible, institutional church.

---

11. von Allmen, "Theological Frame," 15.

12. Though I have used "Nicene" as shorthand in this work, the creed originally adopted at the first council of Nicea in 325 did not include the phrase with these ecclesiological marks. They were added (or another creed including them was affirmed) at the Council of Constantinople in 381. See Davis, *First Seven Ecumenical Councils,* 120–22.

13. Dulles, *Models of the Church,* 123.

14. Dulles, *Models of the Church,* 123.

15. Dulles, *Models of the Church,* 124–25.

How one makes use of these notes will say quite a bit about ecclesiological presuppositions. In *Models of the Church*, Dulles examines how the marks[16] are used differently if one models the church primarily as "institution," "community," "sacrament," "proclamation," or "servant."[17] In what follows, I will show what happens when one views the church and its distinguishing marks through a fundamentally *liturgical* lens.

UNITY

The unity of the church belongs to its deepest nature and calling.[18] It is both gift of grace and aspiration. The Gospel of John records Jesus' "high-priestly" prayer, asking the Father that the church may be one "as we are one, I in them and you in me, that they may be completely one" (John 17:22–23). Likewise, the author of the epistle to the Ephesians pleads for the members of the church to live in unity with one another: "For there is one body and

16. Some theologians make a careful distinction between the terms "notes" of the church and "marks" of the church. The latter points to the use of the adjectives as distinguishing criteria by which a local congregation or denomination may be adjudged to be a "true" or "false" church. The former points to the use of the adjectives as the hopeful description of what the church is meant to be. One might see the first use as the means by which one demarcates a bounded set, and the second use the means by which one centers a set.

17. Dulles notes, for example, that the "proclamation" model does not make much use of the notes at all, and that the "sacrament" model uses the marks quite differently than the "community" model. But the key distinction is between the "institutional" model and all the others. Dulles identifies the institutional model with the bulk of Roman Catholic ecclesiology from the Reformation to Vatican II, and notes that it "identifies the true Church undialectically with a given existing body, which is said to be 'substantially' the Church of Jesus Christ. The other four models by their inner logic tend to depict the attributes of the true Church as ideals that are to a certain extent incarnated in history, thanks to the work of Jesus Christ and the presence of the Holy Spirit in the communities that accept Jesus as Lord. But these ecclesiologies would add that the Church of Jesus Christ is not perfectly realized anywhere on earth, and that any existing ecclesiastical body will only deficiently be the Church of Jesus Christ." In the documents of Vatican II, the Roman Catholic Church moved away from this rigidly institutional model of the church, and in *Lumen Gentium* spoke quite explicitly of the "one, holy, catholic, and apostolic church" as *subsisting in* the (visible, sociological, and describable) Roman Catholic Church rather than making a simple equation between the two. See Dulles, *Models of the Church*, 137–38.

18. Though the four notes stand in line in the creed, highlighting none above the others, our treatment of them will follow von Allmen's thorough treatment of unity, and slightly less thorough treatment of the other adjectives.

one Spirit, just as you were called to the one hope of your calling, one Lord, one faith, one baptism, one God and Father of all, who is above all and through all and in all" (Eph 4:4–5). In a mysterious way, the church is, in fact, and simultaneously strives more fully to be united to Jesus and his Father and to the members of Christ's body (i.e., to one another) through the ministry of the Holy Spirit. Yet, the facts on the ground testify to a church that is deeply fractured and broken[19]—in the words of Samuel John Stone, "oppressed / by schisms rent asunder / by heresies distressed."[20] The division of the church fuels hostility and cynicism within its branches, arouses skepticism and mistrust of its testimony in the world, and undermines the church's ability to fulfill its mission. Thus, one of the great ecclesial developments of the twentieth century is the ecumenical movement, which seeks, in its most ambitious moments, to heal these divisions and, in its less ambitious moments, merely to better understand them.[21]

But what sort of unity do ecumenists seek for the church? And what sort of unity does the church already, if imperfectly, possess? The passage above from Ephesians may identify a few possibilities, which we will see also deployed in von Allmen's work on worship, preaching, and the sacraments.

- The text speaks of "one body," a *relational* unity of the church, its members bearing one another's burdens and regarding one other with the same self-giving love of Christ.

- The text speaks of "one Spirit," a *pneumatological* unity that gifts and inspires and animates the community in its prayer, worship, and service.

- The text speaks of one hope, an *eschatological* unity that summons the church to live into the fullness of the coming reign of God.

---

19. According to the Center for the Study of Global Christianity at Gordon-Conwell Theological Seminary, there are approximately 41,000 Christian denominations and organizations in the world. Of course, such a number is problematic given the difficulty of defining a "denomination." Yet there is no doubt that however we count them, there are some significant number of churches—i.e., more than one—that do not recognize the others as true churches, and therefore demonstrate the church's lack of unity.

20. Stone, "Church's One Foundation."

21. In his farewell lecture to the University of Neuchâtel, in 1980, von Allmen wrote that the hope of the ecumenists is to either "show that the Church's unity is not in fact particularly hurt by its sectarian divisions, or to show instead that unity is constitutive of the Church and must therefore be pursued with every effort." See von Allmen, "Les Marques De L'Église," 97.

- The text speaks of one Lord, a *Christological* unity, as the church is founded by, learns from, is obedient to, and is saved, through the death and resurrection of its gracious master.

- The text speaks of one faith, a *theological* unity, a common understanding of and trust in what has been revealed by God.

- The text speaks of one baptism, which points to a *liturgical* or *sacramental* unity, a common set of practices and rites that embody and rehearse the story of salvation history.

- The text speaks of one calling, a *missional* unity that compels the church to seek justice, serve the lowly, and share the good news of the Gospel.

- And though the text does *not* speak of it, to these types of ecclesial unity one might also add *organizational* unity, by which the church structures itself for obedience, fidelity, and service.

Of course, all these types of unity cannot be neatly distinguished from one another nor is this an exhaustive list, but as we survey von Allmen's writing, we will see how they all find expression in his treatment of the church's worship. As a way of introducing the reader to von Allmen's four main works, the structure of this section will differ from those that follow: we will proceed not by treating each of these types of unity in turn; rather, we will look at von Allmen's primary works to see how ecclesial unity treated in each.

Baptism

In his major book on baptism, *Pastorale du Baptême*, von Allmen notes at the outset that while division in the church is a persistent problem, the sacrament of baptism is a locus where ecumenical conversations have made progress in pursuing ecclesial unity. He appreciatively notes recent interdenominational arrangements of recognition and reciprocity with regard to baptism. He also notes with enthusiasm the efforts to develop "a theology of baptism common to churches belonging to the World Council of Churches and even to the Roman Catholic Church."[22] He rehearses the third-century

---

22. von Allmen, *Pastorale du Baptême*, 8. Here he is pointing to the document (only preliminarily published at the time, 1974) which would become the World Council of Church's *Baptism, Eucharist, and Ministry*.

controversy between Cyprian and Stephen regarding the baptism of con-
verts by those deemed heretics, and comments that the approach of many
churches today echoes Stephen's irenic solution: not to demand a re-baptiz-
ing, but to acknowledge those baptized by an "unrecognized" church into
ecclesial fellowship with the laying on of hands:

> From this practice results, more or less, a situation where unlike
> the Lord's Supper, a source of division, baptism is a major factor
> contributing to the unity of the Church. Consequently, from this
> results a situation that should allow baptism to act as a means to
> accelerate the move toward Christian unity.[23]

To put this in the terms of our categories above, von Allmen here lauds a
recognition in the churches of their pneumatological, Christological, missional, and relational unity, and an increasing theological and sacramental
unity which may eventually lead to some sort of organizational unity.

Various denominational and ecumenical statements—as well as liturgies—identify somewhere between three and six fundamental families of
meaning associated with baptism. In *Pastorale du Baptême*, von Allmen
identifies five basic baptismal themes: 1) unity with the new people of God;
2) anticipation of the last judgment; 3) new birth; 4) virtue and power of
the Holy Spirit; 5) sacrament of faith. The first themes, in particular, speak
explicitly into a discussion of unity.

First, baptism, as the threshold rite of admission into the institutional
church, symbolizes a type of relational unity. This is sometimes articulated
in familial terms, being adopted into the body of Christ, or it may be spoken of sociologically, as the baptized joins God's new people. Those who
are baptized not only join a particular ecclesial community (e.g., Pillar
Church in Holland, Michigan), but they are also joined to the universal
church of Christ—wherever it exists. Baptismal rites typically embody
this dual meaning in a variety of ways: community promises, the presentation of gifts,[24] a blessing of the baptized, a declaration of welcome, etc.
Jean-Jacques von Allmen mentions these last in particular, and, as a way of
enriching the sacramental celebration, combating a "docetic intellectual-

---

23. von Allmen, *Pastorale du Baptême*, II.1.b, 20.

24. At my own home church, each new member is given a framed print of an original
woodcut, "Children of the Light," created by an artist in the church, depicting a circle of
people dancing together. My own children, baptized elsewhere, received a Christ-candle,
which might emphasize more directly the Christological unity rather than relational
unity.

ism," commends to the Reformed churches of Switzerland (and elsewhere?) a liturgical practice familiar to Anglicans and Lutherans as well as Catholics and Orthodox: accompanying the water baptism with the sign of the cross:

> The pastor, immediately after the baptism and before laying hands on the child with the blessing mentioned above, says to the newly baptized individual: "In this way, we welcome you into the family of God, into the Church of Jesus Christ. You now belong to the Lord—here, the officiant can make the sign of the cross on the forehead of the candidate which expresses our belonging to Christ—to serve him all the days of your life."[25]

Actions like these underscore our relational and Christological unity, and when accompanied by statements like the one suggested here, especially the last phrase, they emphasize the missional unity into which children and adults are baptized.

Baptism also signifies a deep Christological unity. The second meaning von Allmen explores is the baptized's paschal connection to Christ in his death and resurrection. He articulates this theme—characteristically—in terms that are eschatological: baptism as the "anticipation of the Last Judgment." In baptism, von Allmen says, we are united to the decisive moment in the history of salvation. One dies with Christ, is buried with Christ, and is raised with Christ.[26] The final judgment has, in some sense, already taken place, a judgment of love, accepted by Jesus as the substitute for humanity's rebellion against God.

The remaining baptismal themes speak with greater richness to others of the Nicene marks and will be treated in due course. But von Allmen also notes the importance of a pneumatological unity signified at baptism by virtue of the gifting and calling of the Holy Spirit. He rehearses the accounts in Acts, where baptism by water and baptism by the Holy Spirit are conferred at different times. He sees in these accounts not so much a two-part baptism or even a prefiguring of the practice of baptism followed by confirmation[27]; rather, he suggests that the key scriptural passage (Acts 8:4–25) is about ecclesial unity and apostolicity, as the baptism by water

25. von Allmen, *Pastorale du Baptême*, 24.

26. von Allmen, *Pastorale du Baptême*, 27.

27. For more on von Allmen's thoughts on confirmation, see von Allmen, *Pastorale du Baptême*, IV.3.b, and von Allmen, *Prophetisme Sacramental*, 140–83.

was conferred by Philip (not an apostle), while the confirming baptism by the Holy Spirit was by Peter and John (both apostles).[28]

Ecclesial unity features prominently in three other discussions relative to baptism. First, in von Allmen's treatment of the "inconveniences" of generalized infant baptism, he wonders whether "indiscriminate infant baptism does not contribute to perpetuating Christian divisions."[29] When baptism goes "without saying" and engrafts an infant into a specific church—the particular local church of his or her family—it reinforces a "confessional fatalism." Better for church unity, he thinks, if a mature, faith-receiving, and faith-owning adult should seek out a denominational home, discerning the best among a welcome number of fitting alternatives.

Second, when von Allmen speaks about the actual *practice* of baptism, he identifies elements of a sacramental or liturgical unity. He first notes that a return to the common practice of the catechumenate—to baptize candidates normally at the Easter Vigil—would further the cause of church unity. Timing it thus would emphasize, he says, the fraternal/relational unity with other churches who are also returning to the ancient practice. It would also emphasize Christological/soteriological unity, highlighting as it does the paschal dying/rising theme of baptismal celebration.[30]

As far as the actual practice and what is required as essential for a *valid* Christian baptism, von Allmen appreciatively cites E. Schlink's succinct summary: "The center, in the celebration of baptism, is the immersion or infusion of the candidate with water while calling upon the name of the Father and the Son and the Holy Spirit."[31] At the same time, von Allmen wishes for a fuller liturgical celebration. While he argues for the helpfulness of other symbolic acts, including anointing, exorcism, the wearing of a white robe, the presentation of a candle, the laying on of hands, and the sign of the Cross,[32] he is content to commend at least the suggestions of the World Council of Churches in *Baptism, Eucharist, and Ministry*, which calls for an explanation of the fundamental meanings of baptism and these practical elements in the rite:

---

28. von Allmen, *Prophetisme Sacramental*, 29–30

29. von Allmen, *Pastorale du Baptême*, III.4.a, 87–88.

30. von Allmen, *Pastorale du Baptême*, IV.1 and IV.8.a, especially IV.8.e, 132–38.

31. Schlink, *Die Lehre von der Taufe*, 27, quoted in von Allmen, *Pastorale du Baptême*, 132.

32. von Allmen, *Pastorale du Baptême*, IV.6.

1) an affirmation of God's initiative in the salvation, of the continuity of his faithfulness, of our total dependence on his grace; 2) an invocation of the Holy Spirit; 3) a renunciation of everything which opposes Christ; 4) a profession of faith in Christ and an adherence to God—Father, Son, and Holy Spirit; 5) a declaration that the baptized person has become a child of God and a witness of the Gospel.[33]

Finally, von Allmen speaks of a unique kind of relational unity—a unity not only with Christ and with fellow members of Christ's body, but even with those who are *not* baptized. One of the responsibilities of the baptized (this might be a "missional unity") is to become "witnesses of life after judgment." He suggests, as the first practice witnessing to life, that baptism is a kind of substitution. In a rather complex sentence, he explains:

Just as in his death and his resurrection—that is, in the baptism in which he had to be baptized—Christ substitutes himself for man's condemnation and opens him to forgiveness and life, so it is then for us that he dies and is resurrected, so Christian baptism does not disconnect from the rest of those who receive it. On the contrary, through their baptism, they represent before God the unbaptized so that the un-baptized can live in the shelter of Christ and those grafted into his body.[34]

Von Allmen hastens to add, "I am aware of the dangers we deal with by venturing in such a direction," but he goes on to say, "A Christian is also baptized for those who are not yet baptized, so as to represent them before God in intercession and thanksgiving." Von Allmen sees this liturgically, in the prayers of the people, and biblically, in the phrase "a royal priesthood"—a people who represent humanity before God. "And one of the most intimate secrets that the Church learns to experience is that because of this representation, it protects the existence of the world itself."[35]

Much more might be said about the unity of the church, especially in connection with baptism. Indeed, Jean-Jacques von Allmen himself said and wrote much more. But his other writings that treat this subject are works of practical theology, which leave liturgical considerations to one

---

33. "La réconciliation des Eglises," quoted in von Allmen, *Pastorale du Baptême.*

34. von Allmen, *Pastorale du Baptême,* conclusion, section 2.

35. I am grateful to Leanne Van Dyk for her work on this aspect of von Allmen's thought, presented in an unpublished paper at the July 2010 meeting of the Association for Reformed and Liturgical Worship.

side, and thus are less helpful for our consideration in this work of liturgical ecclesiology. We move, then, to the first "pole" of normal Lord's Day worship—the act of preaching.

Preaching

For von Allmen, the ministry of preaching is a part of God's salvation history, for "our preaching continues the past preaching of Jesus and looks forward to the Word which He will speak at His return."[36] The Word goes out and gathers in the elect. It gathers them now into the church and will one day gather them into the eschatological reign of God. In this way, preaching has a broad unitive function. It is one of the primary means by which God's people are both called and assembled for worship, and when at worship, built up into the body of Christ.

The common distinction between "missionary" and "liturgical" preaching is explored at some length in both *Preaching & Congregation* as well as in *Worship: Its Theology and Practice*. For von Allmen, the *kerygma* proclaimed "gathers together in all nations and in all ages that eschatological people which is the Church." It does so as an echo of Christ's gathering together of the scattered people of God and as a proleptic precursor to the angels gathering the elect at the end of time. Missionary preaching, as von Allmen calls it, unites the people as it calls them to the font. At the same time, the "threat of dispersion is always present." So the church engages in 'parochial, liturgical preaching' that reproves, rebukes, exhorts, builds up the church, and points to the table as the sacrament of its ongoing unity with the Word.[37]

What sort of unity is it that binds together those who hear and respond to the proclamation of the Word? Using our previously articulated categories, one might see a type of relational unity in preaching, for it is as a united people that we meet God in worship in order to hear and be built up by the Word. One might also identify here a type of pneumatological unity insofar as it is by the call of the Holy Spirit that the dispersed gather to hear the Word of God.[38] There is also a liturgical unity manifest in the preaching of the Word, in the sense that devotion to the "teaching of the apostles" is one of the liturgical elements all Christian churches

36. von Allmen, *Preaching & Congregation*, 7.

37. von Allmen, *Preaching & Congregation*, 9

38. von Allmen, *Preaching & Congregation*, 8. See also von Allmen, *Worship*, 139.

share.[39] That the Word of God proclaimed has such a central place, says von Allmen, is because without it, worship is no longer an encounter with the living God, but merely a monologue. One may see then a Christological unity in the "prophetic" proclamation of the Word,[40] as the people together come face-to-face, as it were, with the Word who is again made flesh in the words of the preacher.[41]

There is also a richer type of relational and theological unity that is especially apparent to those who are called by the church to prepare sermons and to preach them. Sermons, von Allmen argues, are prepared in, with, and for the church, understood rather broadly:

> We cannot be alone in the preparation of a sermon; we are in and with the Church, and it is in order to build her up that we are preparing ourselves. This community which must be created in the preparation of our sermons is a community with God, with the author of the text we are preaching, with the tradition which has stemmed from the text, with the parishioners to whom we are going to preach, and with the world in which the Church has its present being.[42]

Mostly implicit in von Allmen's writing is the theme we have been treating: that preaching demonstrates the unity of the church (or motivates it to greater unity). Yet in one discussion, von Allmen makes this theme explicit. In the last chapter of *Preaching & Congregation*, he argues that the ecumenical movement's pursuit of Christian unity might be helpfully furthered by an approach to preaching treasured in the Reformed church.[43]

39. Whether this is descriptively and historically true or not, von Allmen quotes Acts, the "ancient fathers," Martin Luther, and the Reformed confessions (specifically the Heidelberg) to buttress his own opinion that all churches *should* have the Word of God proclaimed at the heart of their gatherings. See the discussion in von Allmen, *Worship*, 129–30, 145–46.

40. von Allmen distinguishes between the "clerical" proclamation of the Word (divine discourse as expressed in the greeting, absolution, blessing, etc.), its reading within the service, and the "prophetic" proclamation, which is preaching. See von Allmen, *Worship*, 130.

41. Here, von Allmen leans on the Helvetic maxim: "The Preaching of the Word of God is the Word of God." See discussion in von Allmen, *Worship*, 12–14.

42. von Allmen, *Preaching & Congregation*, 49. In the pages that follow, von Allmen gives some practical suggestions for preachers to nurture this unity, such as identifying a few people in the congregation and having those specific individuals and their circumstances of trial or triumph in mind as one prepares.

43. Jean-Jacques von Allmen does not necessarily see "the preaching that builds up"

Reviewing his argument, there will sound notes of Christological, theological, and organizational unity.

Ecumenical conversations, von Allmen argues, have focused on the sacraments, on church polity, and—when it focuses on proclamation of the Word—on "missionary" preaching. There is hardly any mention of preaching that builds up, "as though it had no essential role in our struggle for Christian unity."[44] Of course, missionary preaching, he argues, is valuable in the church's quest for greater unity: "Missionary preaching is essentially a work of Christian unification, since it binds all the faithful to the living Lord; since, by proclaiming the crucifixion and resurrection of Christ, it brings them into contact with the central and decisive event in the history of the world."[45] Yet "parochial" preaching (i.e., the preaching that builds up) aims at *preserving* that unity—defending and reinforcing it. It does this in three ways.

First, it proclaims unequivocally that the church is one because she has only one Lord. It is an idolatrous scandal when anything that might be used to guide us to Christ and his witness is misused in a way that usurps Christ's central place. Neither the means of grace themselves nor the fruits of grace; neither the Bible, nor the sacraments, nor music, nor our neighbor; neither faith itself, nor conversion, nor the saints, nor the church's dogma, are central. For von Allmen, the church is one because she has only one Lord, and preaching, which builds up, "dismisses from the center of church life anything which might occupy the place of Christ, and hence anything which might divide the church instead of uniting it."[46] He suggests that the Reformed churches can call upon the other churches in the ecumenical movement to take more seriously the preaching that builds up, not as a competitor to an emphasis on mission or the sacraments but rather as a means of "gaining greater respect for the lordship of Christ."[47]

The second way preaching that builds up might contribute to unity in ecumenical conversations is the way in which it speaks specifically to a central ecumenical concern: unity in diversity. The debate on the nature of

---

as the unique or distinctive *gift* of the Reformed churches to the larger universal church. But it is a characteristic strength of the Reformed churches, he says, to sense and appreciate "the miraculous character of preaching, its status as an eschatological event." See his discussion in von Allmen, *Preaching & Congregation*, 59–68, esp. 64.

44. von Allmen, *Preaching & Congregation*, 59.

45. von Allmen, *Preaching & Congregation*, 59.

46. von Allmen, *Preaching & Congregation*, 59.

47. von Allmen, *Preaching & Congregation*, 60.

the unity of the church, says von Allmen, is marked by Protestant fears of a squelching of necessary diversity. Roman Catholics, on the other hand, fear a multiplicity of sects compromising the oneness of the church. There is a parallel problem—a similar tension between exegesis and creed, as a remarkable diversity within the canonical witness still tells one kerygmatic gospel story: "We must allow each of scriptural witness to express its own particular character, but each of these canonical witnesses must also be integrated in the single confession and adoration of Jesus Christ." In the same way, von Allmen says, a solution modeled on preaching would allow for a variety of "human responses to the Gospel message" while affirming that this variety is permissible "only within certain universally recognized limits."[48]

The third contribution the Reformed tradition might make to the ecumenical discourse, according to von Allmen, is in conversations surrounding preaching, mutual recognition of ministry, and the apostolicity of other churches. His argument is this: Ministry, that is, the selection of particular individuals to help the church be her true self, is a divine gift and right. That ministry consists not only in the valid celebration of the sacraments but also in the right proclamation of the Word. Reformed Christians ought to be less afraid to claim apostolicity in a concrete historical form (and thus move away from what he calls a type of "illuminism.") At the same time, Reformed Christians can bring to the ecumenical table, so to speak, an insistence that:

> the question of the authorization of the ministry should be extended to include the ministry of the Word as preached, and secondly, in consequence of this, that a criterion for apostolic succession should be faithfulness in translating and making present the apostolic witness.[49]

48. Given von Allmen's place in the ecumenical conversations of his day, he was surely not naïve about the difficulties in discerning what these "universally recognized limits" might be. Yet at this point and in this work he does not offer much more detail to point the way forward, other than to extend the metaphor in a rhetorically interesting but not altogether helpful way: "What limits the diversity of the canonical witnesses is their reference to the Word of God incarnate in Jesus Christ. . . . In the same way what should limit the variety of human responses is that in all of them one ought to recognize the signs of the true church: not necessarily the same traditions but the same canon of traditions; not necessarily the same dogmatics, but the same dogmas; not necessarily the same liturgies but the same sacraments; not necessarily the same discipline but the same ethic" (von Allmen, *Preaching & Congregation*, 61–62).

49. von Allmen, *Lord's Supper*, 63.

We turn now to the second "pole" of the regular Lord's Day worship service, the heart of the "Jerusalemite" phase—the Lord's Supper—to discern how the church's unity is expressed, shaped, and nurtured there.

The Lord's Supper

To a fractious group of Christians in Corinth, St. Paul, appealing for unity, pointed to the table and the meal shared there: "The bread that we break, is it not a sharing in the body of Christ? Because there is one bread, we who are many are one body, for we all partake of the one bread" (1 Cor 10:17). Paul puts at the center of things the Christological basis for the church's unity and its relational consequence. Here, the vertical and horizontal aspects of *koinonia* reinforce one another. As with baptism, these deep aspects of Christian unity have the potential to come to fruition in more obvious types of unity: theological, sacramental, and even organizational. Yet in contrast to the font, which is a place of promise for both manifesting church unity and pursuing it, the table is a place where the church's unity is both most deeply sensed and most deeply threatened: "It is not surprising that the Supper should be the final test of peace and unity in the church . . . it is over the celebration and interpretation of the Supper that dogmatic and canonical divisions are most evident."[50]

The loss of ecclesial unity over the "celebration and interpretation of the Supper" is a story told by many,[51] and von Allmen alludes to it in his central work on the Eucharist, *The Lord's Supper*. Summarizing some of the current (in his day) historical and textual scholarship concerning the development of the Lord's Supper as an ecclesiological rite,[52] he acknowledges that there was significant diversity in both practice and understanding. But this observed diversity did not, at least at first, "compromise the unity of the church."[53] That is to say, even its organizational unity was not harmed, insofar as it did not prevent one church from recognizing another local church as church, even though its liturgical tradition or interpretation of the meal was different. Furthermore, says von Allmen, this unity persisted

50. von Allmen, *Lord's Supper*, 9.

51. For some current examples, see Foley, *From Age to Age*; Kilmartin, *Eucharist in the West*; and Bradshaw, *Eucharistic Origins*. For a complexifying voice, see McGowan, *Rethinking Eucharistic Origins*, 173–91.

52. von Allmen, *Lord's Supper*, 10–14

53. von Allmen, *The Lord's Supper*, 14.

for a thousand years: there were no violent controversies concerning the Eucharist during the first millennium of the church. It was only after the schisms of the eleventh and sixteenth centuries that theologians 'found' in the writings of the church's theologians of the first millennium contrasting positions on, for example, the understanding of Christ's real presence at the meal or the proper place for the epiclesis. They then used what they found to support their own understandings or practices. The supper, von Allmen says, "fits ill into a divided church, since division calls into question one of its special purposes: unity."[54]

For von Allmen, these two facts—an underlying Christological and relational unity alongside theological, liturgical, and eventually organizational diversity—suggest that Eucharistic theology[55] does not merely admit of multiple interpretive approaches but rather *requires* it. In fact, disunity, he fears, can isolate one particular element of the Eucharistic life and in that isolation and imbalance, lean toward distortion and heresy. By way of solution, he points toward a theology of Eucharistic complementarity:

> I wonder, however, if it is not true that Eucharistic theology . . . is a theology of complementary rather than contradictory alternatives and even a synthesis of elements so diverse that if they became mutually exclusive they would threaten the Christian supper with dire peril.[56]

Even so, while there will always be a fitting "here-and-now"-ness, culturally, to the church's Eucharistic celebrations, it is unity that will have the last word, because the Lord's Supper makes the church aware of her eschatological nature, the coming reign of God, and her solidarity with other Christians[57] awaiting the parousia.

The divisions in manner of celebration and understanding of the Lord's Supper proliferated after the Reformation, notes von Allmen, yet the fundamental disunity he sees is not theological or ceremonial, but liturgical. That is to say, von Allmen locates the most significant historical

54. von Allmen, *Lord's Supper*, 16. One might dispute von Allmen's claims about "violent controversies" and the unity of the church in the first millennium, but his theological observation about the meal serving the purpose of unity seems quite robust on both biblical and theological grounds.

55. Here, von Allmen might well affirm the distinction between *theologia prima* and *theologia secunda,* and argue for the importance of diversity and complementarity in both understanding and practice.

56. von Allmen, *Lord's Supper*, 17.

57. von Allmen, *Lord's Supper*, 40.

fracture in the church to those bodies after the Reformation who divided not one group from another, but who separated the Lord's Supper from the Lord's Day. Acknowledging that this division was the product of tension between realizing the "unreality" of a Lord's Supper—in which the laity did not participate at all—and realizing, pastorally, that a laity accustomed to communing only once per year could not quickly move to weekly Communion. The various compromise positions (once per month, once per quarter, at major festivals, etc.) quickly became permanent, and the hope for an increased frequency of celebration was never realized.[58]

From von Allmen's point of view, this separation of the supper from worship "divided the church more radically than any of the previous schisms."[59] It produced two distinct "types" of Christianity—a "Catholic" type and a Protestant type, the latter of which is a *sentire ecclesiam*, a movement of ideas, which does not "exclude the sacramental life, but remains on the fringe of it."[60] As a consequence, it is much more difficult now to work towards organizational ecclesial unity because these two "types" of Christianity experience and articulate their Christological and relational unity so differently; the former foundationally in the sacrament, the latter foundationally in the proclamation of the Word. Members of these two camps, says von Allmen, have difficulty "acknowledging, on the surface or in depth, their own church life in the life of another."[61]

Despite these difficulties, which von Allmen mentions at the outset of *The Lord's Supper*, there remains a profound unity that is exercised in the celebration of the Eucharist. "There is," he says, "no more triumphant challenge to fragmentation, to neglect, to dispersal, to the sectaries, to everything which is diabolical . . . than the character of the supper."[62] He speaks quite explicitly of the Christological, Relational, and Pneumatological aspects of this unity. When the church meets Christ at the supper, he says, quoting Augustine, it is the "total Christ" who is present, head and body. His emphasis on salvation history is evident as he speaks about the church's unity with "the Christ who came, the Christ who reigns, and the Christ who is coming."[63] Further, because Christ is present, his whole body is present, the whole communion

58. von Allmen, *Lord's Supper*, 17–18.

59. von Allmen, *Lord's Supper*, 18.

60. von Allmen, *Lord's Supper*, 18.

61. von Allmen, *Lord's Supper*, 18.

62. von Allmen, *Lord's Supper*, 47.

63. von Allmen, *Lord's Supper*, 47.

of saints "in whom the history of salvation is accomplished," in a prefiguring of the eschatological ingathering of the people of God. Finally, because of the Holy Spirit, relational or fraternal unity is the inevitable result of Christological unity: "Communion with Christ assumes and demands that those who, because of their union with Christ, are of one Spirit with Him should form one body among themselves."[64] Further, he argues that absent this fraternal or relational communion, it is legitimate to question the Christological unity that binds the church to Christ. Thus, he commends the "classical" epiclesis that invokes the Spirit upon both the elements and upon the people, that they both might become the body of Christ.[65]

These aspects of the church's unity all find liturgical expression at various points in the Eucharistic rite. The kiss of peace, von Allmen suggests, is a liturgical attestation to the church's relational unity. It is a renunciation of everything else in the world that might be a source of opposition and division. At the sanctus the church joins in a unified song of adoration. There is also the epiclesis, which centrally petitions God to make the church one. Though there is great variety in the particulars of this prayer in practice, von Allmen notes the fittingness especially of the phrases borrowed from ancient sources[66] which speak of grain and grapes gathered together from many fields and hills to become the one loaf and cup, just as the church is gathered "from the four corners of the earth . . . to make all the baptized of past, present, and future into a community conscious of its destiny, unity, and mission."[67] This is perhaps the most important moment in the service for von Allmen, and he notes that in an age of substantial ecumenical exertion,[68] this epiclesis

---

64. von Allmen, Lord's Supper, 55. See also von Allmen, Lord's Supper, 59.

65. von Allmen, Lord's Supper, 60.

66. von Allmen mentions in particular the Apostolic Tradition of Hippolytus and John Calvin's paraphrase of the Didache.

67. von Allmen, Lord's Supper, 60.

68. In The Lord's Supper, von Allmen devotes a number of pages to the ecumenical problem of "intercommunion." On pages 66–72, he writes of the history of division within the churches as a result of mutual excommunication, differences in interpretation of what happens at the Supper, disagreements over presidency at the table, and the proliferation of new groups in missionary lands. In the end, he wonders how one congregation keeps another from coming to the table, one who is welcome at another church, "without refusing to recognize that church as Church." He believes it is because we do not find, by and large, the arguments to exclude others, the arguments which birthed schism, to be persuasive any longer. And so while he does address some of the tensions surrounding denominational practices of 'open' communion, open tables at ecumenical sessions, or temporary 'pan-denominational churches,' he thinks these are, at best, stop-gap

reminds us that true unity is "not within human grasp, that it can only come in answer to prayer."[69]

Underscoring this point in the conclusion, von Allmen wonders again how we speak of the Supper as a sacrament of Christian unity in the face of the church's deep divisions. His response is that we must "first speak of the unity of the Supper itself." By this he means to point to all the various meanings and purposes of the Eucharist—thanksgiving, communion, commemoration, sacrifice, and mystery—meanings which he has elucidated in the previous chapters in six dialectic poles. All these meanings must be held in unity, simultaneity, and balance:

> If in the divided Church the Supper is again to become the factor and motive of unity which it really is, then it must be allowed to recover the fullness and the balance of its unity. And this must happen in each Church; when it does it will bring about a radical reform in each of them.[70]

The first task for the separated churches, then, is to "rediscover the meaning of the Eucharist" and to "give it the place which belongs to it."[71] At the same time, the unitive virtue of what von Allmen calls the "Eucharistic event" does not come through an appropriate understanding of the meal, nor does it come through its fitting ritual celebration. He therefore does not offer a single theological interpretation but rather a multivalent exposition of its many meanings. Likewise, he does not offer much in way of particular recommendations for practice—for example, he does not weigh in on the relative value of communing by intinction in a common cup verses communing individually in pews via small cups of wine.[72] No, we pray for unity

measures and at worst, ways for the churches to avoid becoming Church. In other words, the only solution to the "problem" of intercommunion is communion. The experience of unity—christological and relational—must necessarily lead to organizational unity: "If the Eucharist is the seal of unity which has been realized, it is also a factor in the unity which is to be realized" (von Allmen, *Lord's Supper*, 69). Compare this to the Anglican N.T. Wright, who commends first intercommunion that we might indeed see and own the insignificance of the causes of our organizational division. See Wright, *The Meal Jesus Gave Us*.

69. von Allmen, *Lord's Supper*, 60.

70. von Allmen, *Lord's Supper*, 114.

71. Though von Allmen is speaking to all church traditions here, he is speaking with an especially critical—if loving—voice to his own Reformed sisters and brothers.

72. This is a bit unusual, as he is not shy elsewhere to both praise or critique particular liturgical practices. (For example, he gasps in horror at the baptismal practice wherein a rose is dipped into the water in the font and the water is thence sprinkled on the infant.

at the table, and we find it there because of God's action, because it is "instituted by Christ and quickened by the Holy Spirit."[73]

Having surveyed von Allmen's comments on preaching and the sacraments, in conclusion, we now turn more generally to the Lord's Day worship and the components of the cult which further exercise and give expression to the church's unity.

Worship

The body of Christ—gathered, in order to worship, in a particular time and space—manifests a number of aspects of ecclesial unity we have already been considering. Though von Allmen does not use this schema, we will see signs of theological, relational, Christological, eschatological, liturgical, and organizational unity in our exploration of his writing on worship.

The most obvious manifestation of the church's unity is in the fact of the liturgical gathering itself, which brings disparate and sometimes desperate people together. Speaking about the necessity and usefulness of worship, von Allmen points to a deep relational and eschatological unity, grounded in their Christological unity. He says that the cult gives to its members "the deepest cohesion, the most basic solidarity which can be found on this earth."[74] But it is not only church members "on this earth" who join in unity at worship. Because worship is an eschatological event, it manifests an eschatological unity, unfettered by limitations of space and time. The whole history of salvation is summed up in Christ; thus all those whom he has saved are also present at worship. "Therefore, the cult is preeminently the moment of true community: all those who are hidden with Christ in God are present. . . . Christian worship is the most emphatic contradiction of human solitude and abandonment."[75]

Those gathered include not only the baptized present in a particular congregation but also "the elect wherever they are situated." This includes those prevented from worshipping by illness or travel difficulties (or other, perhaps less excusable reasons). It also includes those "gathered in other places of worship to celebrate the same cult, absent in body but present in

---

See von Allmen, *Pastorale du Baptême*, n652.)

73. von Allmen, *Lord's Supper*, 116.
74. von Allmen, *Worship*, 119.
75. von Allmen, *Worship*, 198.

Spirit."[76] Present are also the saints of ages past, those "hidden with Christ in God," whose images are seen in many sanctuaries: von Allmen mentions the nave of the church of St. Apollinaris of Ravenna;[77] I think of the beautiful tapestries at the Cathedral of the Angels in Los Angeles. Elsewhere, von Allmen points to the supernatural realm, discussing the "angels, partners in worship" when he speaks of those who are "participants in worship,"[78] albeit primarily as witnesses. The circle is drawn more broadly still when von Allmen explores the ways in which the whole world "and its sighs" are united in worship[79] in a way that has cosmic implications: as worship "stabilizes the world, penetrating it with something which opposes its fragmentation and contends with its chaos."[80] Thus, the relational unity of the church expands into an eschatological unity, as more and more are drawn in, even in representative ways, by the church's worship.

This unity finds explicit expression at various points in the worship service, some of which have already been mentioned, associated with the sacraments and preaching. Von Allmen also points to other prayers that declare the unity of the church come together in adoration:

> In all confessions, the liturgies constantly declare this, and if here I quote only a few prayers which figure in the Reformed liturgies, it is to emphasize that this assured transcendence of space in Christian worship is not peculiar to churches of a catholic type: "We praise Thee together with all those Christians who are assembled today," says the Liturgy of Oostervald of 1713. "Bless, O Lord, the worship we come to render to Thee, in communion with all Thy Church gathered together this day," says the Liturgy of Neuchâtel of 1904; and according to the *Liturgie jurassienne* of 1955, the Sanctus is chanted "with the angels and all the powers of

---

76. Interestingly, von Allmen notes the possibility of worship services transmitted by radio and television and the possibility that these will include still larger groups in the unity of those gathered to worship. He does not rule out the usefulness of such tools for evangelism and catechesis, but finds them inadequate for worship because they may degrade worship to the "level of a spectacle or a lecture." More importantly, watching a television broadcast of a worship service (or, presumably, streaming one on the internet) lacks "brotherly fellowship, and above all the possibility of communicating with the body and blood of Christ" (von Allmen, *Worship,* 211).

77. von Allmen, *Worship,* 198.

78. von Allmen, *Worship,* 205–9.

79. von Allmen, *Worship,* 209–12.

80. von Allmen, *Worship,* 120.

the heavens, with the spirits of just men made perfect, and with all the Church militant here in earth."[81]

In addition to prayers like these, von Allmen mentions a number of other moments in a typical Lord's Day service in which the unity of the church is both expressed and strengthened. For example, he speaks of the opening greeting as a time of "brotherly encouragement at the moment when we are to appear before the terrible face of the Lord, and, in addition, the proof of spiritual cohesion and solidarity."[82] Congregational singing, too, helps to "give ordered form to exultation, canalize it, and above all, enable all the faithful to share it."[83] We recall here John Calvin's sense that the preferred way to join prayer and music in worship was congregational singing *in unison* because of its unitive character.[84] In all its prayers, spoken and sung, says von Allmen, the church is presented before God as "a fellowship of persons" and thus, for the congregation to own the prayer as its own, it is fitting that they say a closing "Amen."[85]

These prayers all offer a type of relational unity and may also point indirectly to theological unity. The creed, however, is the most significant moment when the church's doctrinal unity comes to the fore; when it confesses together what it believes, and "united in faith, hope, and love, responds to the Word of God by its own words."[86] Von Allmen identifies other elements in worship which evince the church's *koinonia*, and point to its unity: its missional unity in the offertory; its relational and pneumatological unity when it offers "mutual exhortations and encouragements" to one another; and even the "notices," which he recommends placing just before the prayers of intercession, so that the congregation might remember that after its dispersal on Sunday, it remains a united group under God's

---

81. von Allmen, *Worship*, 198. For more on the *sanctus* as a locus of unity, see von Allmen, *Worship*, 162.

82. von Allmen, *Worship*, 173.

83. von Allmen, *Worship*, 170.

84. For his part, von Allmen, along with Calvin, notes that he would prefer singing that is majestic and reverent—like Gregorian chant—but fit for the vernacular language of worshippers (rather than Latin). He does not object, he writes, to Lutheran chorales, Huguenot psalms, and what he calls "Jordanian melodies" (African-American spirituals). However, he is *not* a fan of "Anglo-Saxon revivalist hymns which, all in all, are a betrayal of the cultural responsibilities of Christian worship." von Allmen, *Worship*, 91.

85. von Allmen, *Worship*, 159.

86. von Allmen, *Worship*, 168.

"watchful gaze."[87] Finally, von Allmen commends an uncommon practice: the kiss of peace, taking place just before the preface or after the Lord's prayer or after the offertory. It was taken for granted in apostolic times, he says, as a "sign of mutual reconciliation and unity."[88] In all these ways, says von Allmen, "the church shows in its cult that it is but one heart and one soul (Acts 2:32), since it has the canticles, the Amens, the confession of faith, the Lord's Prayer, the offertory, and above all, Holy Communion as proof."[89]

One other aspect of ecclesial unity warrants comment here: liturgical unity. Roman Catholics, for example, locate one aspect of ecclesial unity in the fixed liturgy which all congregations celebrate, no matter their cultural location. This unity was even more pronounced prior to Vatican II,[90] when that liturgical uniformity extended to the universal mandated use of Latin as the language of liturgical celebration.[91] To this point, von Allmen notes that third century worship was quite different from that in the seventh century, and worship in Egypt looked different than that offered in Gaul. These variations, he says, "do not compromise the basic unity of the cult and of the Church, even if the points of difference are often not inconsiderable." Indeed, variety of expression is not only legitimate, it is "necessary, since the cult is not only the expression of the Church itself but also the expression of such and such a Church situated in time and space."[92] At the same time, that variety of expression has limits. The use of different lectionaries, the position of the Lord's Prayer in the service, the use of fixed or extempo-

87. von Allmen, *Worship*, 171–76.

88. von Allmen, *Worship*, 175.

89. von Allmen, *Worship*, 175.

90. This story is too complex to detail here. Liturgical uniformity was not earnestly pursued in the Roman Church until after the 2nd Gregorian Reform under Leo VII. It was given new life in the counter-reformation. See Wainwright and Tucker, *Oxford History of Christian Worship*, 223, 251; White, *Roman Catholic Worship*.

91. See, for example, Pope Pius XII in *Mediator Dei*: "The use of the Latin language prevailing in a great part of the church affords at once an imposing sign of unity and an effective safeguard against the corruptions of true doctrine" (Pius XII, *Mediator Dei*, 60). Jean-Jacques von Allmen acknowledges the desire to mark the unity of the church in time and space through the adoption of a single liturgical language (Latin). Yet he quotes the Second Helvetic Confession and its insistence on use of vernacular, a language understood by all. Insistence on Latin is not so much about *unity*, he says, as it is an insistence on maintaining "the separation between the clergy who are familiar with the language and the laity who are not" (von Allmen, *Worship*, 101).

92. von Allmen, *Worship*, 284.

raneous prayers, kneeling or not kneeling—all of these are legitimate. What he finds illegitimate is the abandonment, especially in certain Protestant families, of the basic rhythm of worship in two phases: apostolic witness (preaching) and Communion. We have no right, he says, to "confirm our confessional liturgical peculiarities in their most notorious features, that is, in their breaking of the normal rhythm of Christian worship."[93] No, the church's unity is best served and expressed when God and God's people meet at the table: "Worship is the moment of encounter and unity between the Lord and His people who give themselves to each other, receive each other, in the joy and liberty of Communion."[94]

Summary

We have identified a number of aspects of ecclesial unity that von Allmen treats in his writings on preaching, worship, and the sacraments. Among them are pneumatological, eschatological, Christological, theological, liturgical, missional, and organizational unity. At this point, two concluding comments are necessary regarding the two least-developed themes: organizational unity and missional unity.

For von Allmen, the key implication for pursuing ecclesial unity is the re-establishment of a regular pattern of weekly Eucharistic celebration in Protestant churches—so that their worship might in structure align with the Roman Catholic and Orthodox Churches as well as the broad and deep history of the church's tradition, grounded, as he believes, in the biblical model of Jesus' liturgical life. The last section of this work will return to this theme. At the same time, one of the objectives for which ecumenists are often striving—an organizational unity—is perhaps the least interesting or significant in a *liturgical* ecclesiology. Von Allmen says as much in *Preaching & Congregation* when, in discussing problems that beset the goal of mutual recognition, he says, "considerations which carry the most weight today are those with the least specifically theological value."[95]

Interestingly, and perhaps distressingly, von Allmen gave little value to articulating the *missional* aspects of the church's unity—i.e., the way in which the church is united in its calling to the world. There is little mention of how the church's vocation to love and serve "the least of these," to

93. von Allmen, *Worship*, 287.

94. von Allmen, *Worship*, 207.

95. von Allmen, *Preaching & Congregation*, 63.

pursue justice and peace in the world, to join God's work in the world, finds expression and nurture in its weekly worshipping life. There are hints of that calling in von Allmen's treatment of the church's preaching ministry, a ministry that includes the proclamation of the *kerygma* to the unbaptized. And there are other hints in von Allmen's sense that the church is united in mission simply by virtue of its holiness—i.e., its standing apart from the world and offering in its worship both threat and promise to it. However, von Allmen has more to say in a corollary area—missional apostolicity— and we will return to some of these themes in that section below.

HOLINESS

Gordon Lathrop places two sentences from the ancient liturgy of Jerusalem at the heart of his three-volume project in liturgical theology. "Holy things for holy people," says the presider. The people respond: "One is holy, one is Lord, Jesus Christ."[96] In this exchange, the relationship between Jesus Christ, the people who worship him, and the things they use, do, and say in order to worship are all connected through the theological concept of holiness. What is holiness and what does it mean to attribute holiness to the church, or for the church to attribute holiness to God, to scripture, to water, wine, bread, speech, time, space, or anything else? Jean-Jacques von Allmen's treatment of holiness is much briefer than his treatment of unity, reviewed above.[97] His books on preaching and on the Lord's Supper have little to say about the subject, though they do name as sacred some of the things just mentioned: the Trinity, Communion, scripture, and so forth. However, the eponymous chapter in his important collection, *Prophétisme Sacramental*, does address the church's holiness, and von Allmen takes up the theme at various points in his primary work on worship and in his book on the sacrament of baptism, the central liturgical mark of holiness.

As with the previous discussion, it will be helpful to discern in von Allmen a number of interrelated theological aspects of the subject in view. Thus, what follows explores four ways of thinking about holiness:

96. See the facing title page in Lathrop, *Holy Things*; for a key discussion of this passage, see Lathrop, *Holy Things*, 133–38.

97. Likewise, his treatment of catholicity and apostolicity are also less developed than his treatment of the church's unity, as we will see.

- Holiness as separation, clearly distinguishing the sacred from the profane.

- Holiness as perfection, marked by an actual or aspirational purity or piety.

- Holiness as dedication, identifying something as especially fit for God's use to do something.

- Holiness as representation, by which other things are made or declared holy.

Our discussion will be divided into four brief sections, treating each of these in turn. It will be preceded by some preliminary remarks on the source of the church's holiness, and concluded with a summary section on liturgical markers of holiness.

Source of Holiness

Avery Dulles suggests that holiness is perhaps the oldest of the four ecclesial attributes, found in the Apostles' Creed as well as the Nicene. But if the church is holy, what is the source of this sanctification? In the creeds it is closely connected with the Holy Spirit. Dulles cites Pierre Nautin's conviction that the original clause from the Apostles' Creed was probably *credo in spiritum sanctum in sanctam ecclesiam*—I believe in the Holy Spirit in the holy church.[98] In *Doxology*, Geoffrey Wainwright makes a Trinitarian argument that the church's holiness comes from its identity as the people of God, the body of Christ, and the temple of the Holy Spirit.[99] Von Allmen, on the other hand, focuses fundamentally on the role of Jesus Christ when he speaks of the church's holiness. He certainly acknowledges the role of the Spirit as the source of *worship*, transplanting people into an eschatological world, making "the world to come present here and now."[100] It is also the Holy Spirit who sanctifies the stuff of worship—word and water and bread and wine, as the sacramental and sacrificial "instruments of salvation."[101] But when von Allmen speaks in his central book on worship concerning the

98. Dulles, *Models*, 124.

99. Wainwright, *Doxology*, 127. This is, Wainwright notes, the same structure used by Lesslie Newbigin in *Household of God*.

100. von Allmen, "Worship and the Holy Spirit," 125.

101. von Allmen, "Worship and the Holy Spirit," 128.

source of the church's holiness, it is a sanctification provided by Christ and his perfect worship. Citing 1 Peter 1 and Hebrews 10, von Allmen asserts that it is Christ's holiness, the purity of the "spotless lamb," which protects and prefigures the church's worship, setting up "as it were a screen, behind which and in whose shelter" the community worships and the world continues to exist, "safe from the threat of destruction God declared against the sin of Adam."[102] The church's worship is holy because it engages in worship that is a memorial and effective echo of Christ's worship. The church is holy because Christ is holy.

Differentiation

A first aspect of holiness is separation. Things and people that are declared holy are set apart, distinct from the rest of the world.[103] A central theme of von Allmen's liturgical ecclesiology is how the church exists in relation to the world as both threat and promise. This threat and promise is distilled in its worship and, in particular, at baptism, where the church and the world, the sacred and the profane, are distinguished from one another:

> By its cult and in its cult, the Church becomes manifest and aware of itself, first of all, as a baptismal community. This amounts to saying in the first place that the cult differentiates the Church from the world. In worship, "the Church emerges, without pretentiousness but firmly, out of the profanity of the environment in which it is normally immersed" (Barth, *Dogmatics*). It shows that it is not of the world, and that, in consequence, the only justification for its temporal existence is to offer worship.[104]

The church's worship makes plain that the church is not any human organization, but rather the people called and elected by God. They are the ones who respond to the appeal of the Gospel, walking the path of death and new life with and in Christ.[105]

This distinction is not welcomed everywhere in the church. There are those who are suspicious of it, says von Allmen. Some are suspicious because of a theological misunderstanding of the incarnation, supposing that in God's reconciliation with humans in Christ, the distinction has become

102. von Allmen, *Worship*, 24.
103. See, for example, Deut 7:6; 1 Pet 2:9.
104. von Allmen, *Worship*, 45.
105. von Allmen, *Worship*, 45. See also von Allmen, *Worship*, 57–61.

anachronistic. There are those who mistrust the distinction because of a post-Constantinian atrophy of baptismal discipline, when the sacramental sign of the distinction between church and world has been co-opted (as it has been in the west) by the state or culture at large. Some are distrustful of the distinction because of impatience, wishing to manifest here and now the fullness of the church's catholicity without passing "through the narrow gate of holiness."[106] Finally, there is a distrust of the distinction that is based in a docetism that "refuses to believe that the sacred can truly disclose its presence in earthly life."[107] The common thread to all these mistrusts and misunderstandings, says von Allmen, is a "lowering of eschatological tension," a collapse of the age to come into the present age. This was especially characteristic of the church in the era of "historic Christianity" or Christendom, where the church was tempted to think of the world either as a defeated, declawed opponent or an ally. Yet in the post-Christian situation in which we now find ourselves, in which Christians are a minority group, it is all the more important, says von Allmen, for the church to robustly reclaim its other-ness. "Pietism," he writes, "is for the Church the very condition of its mission to the world"[108] as both threat and promise.

Perfection

The second aspect of holiness von Allmen addresses is perfection or purity. This quality may be inherent or imputed or aspired to. The church is set apart to be holy and to be made perfect. This is especially apparent in that ritual cleansing is among the central liturgical antecedents for baptism, the primary liturgical marker of the church's holiness. Many passages in Leviticus and Numbers highlight this aspect of the holiness of God's people, based on what they do or touch. The people must submit to a ritual cleansing in order to enter into God's presence.[109] Sacrificial animals were to be spotless,[110] even as Christ was the spotless lamb,[111] and the church Christ's spotless bride.[112] In Ephesians 1:4, holiness is linked directly to be-

106. von Allmen, *Worship*, 60.

107. von Allmen, *Worship*, 60.

108. von Allmen, *Worship*, 61.

109. von Allmen, *Pastoral du Baptême*, 10.

110. See, for example, Deut 17:1.

111. See 1 Pet 1:19.

112. See Rev 19:1.

ing "blameless." Thus, many discussions of holiness focus on this aspect—specifically, on the ethical implications of being a separate people. This is Wainwright's approach, for example, as his treatment of holiness in *Doxology* is fundamentally about the problem of post-baptismal sin.[113]

Indeed, post-baptismal sin is a problem since, despite the church's identity as a "holy people," having passed through the cleansing and sanctifying waters of baptism, the church remains manifestly *not* blameless or absent of sin, either in its individuals or as an institution. It should be a community marked by love and justice, mercy and reconciliation, generosity and thanksgiving, righteousness and peace. Yet it is not. Von Allmen says that this is so because baptism, the threshold of holiness, "effected no more than a sacramental transference," i.e., a transference of Christ's holiness to the church. Even though members of the church are indeed holy, "they have yet to become what they are." Their holiness can be "compromised or even annulled by the indolence of those who are its beneficiaries, their failure to demonstrate its effectiveness in their lives (see 1 Cor 10:1–13).[114] This is particularly a problem for those in the Roman Catholic church, says von Allmen, where baptized infant members of the church, once grown, are technically but not actually required to keep a "moral behavior which comes into open conflict with what is commonly done around them."[115] Baptism is thus a very serious matter for the church, and von Allmen advocates strongly for a recovery of more robust baptismal discipline and a more consistent baptismal practice as a marker of both God's electing activity and the response of faith that leads to greater sanctification. These recommendations will be examined in greater detail below.

Dedication

Holiness involves not simply being set apart, but being set apart *for a purpose*. Part of that purpose is indeed to be or become perfect. But that purpose is also to carry out a mission, to follow a calling, to *do* something. For

---

113. When Wainwright turns to liturgical implications, he spends most of his time, therefore, on the sacrament of penance and corporate confession in worship. He also makes the argument that the Eucharist is the pre-eminent occasion for Christian self-judgment (there is threat and promise again) by which baptismal judgment is renewed. See Wainwright, *Doxology*, 127–32.

114. von Allmen, *Worship*, 65.

115. von Allmen, *Pastorale du Baptême*, 8.

example, von Allmen will assert that in preaching, human words are made holy for a purpose; they are "chosen, justified, and sanctified by God in order to communicate his own Word."[116] Ecclesiologists will differ in their emphases on what the church as a whole is called to do. Some will emphasize evangelism. Some will focus on a "social gospel"—i.e., deeds of justice and mercy in the world. Others will highlight solidarity with and liberation for the downtrodden. Others will accentuate the church's call to mutual encouragement and love within the body of Christ. The next section on the church's activity will explore von Allmen's writing about ecclesial activity in more depth. For now, it is enough to note that for him, the fundamental activities of the church all flow from and back into its central activity: worship.

Representation

The final aspect of holiness von Allmen explores is representative holiness. That is to say, "the Church, the Body of Christ, the sacerdotal people, fulfills in the world a mediatorial function."[117] In von Allmen's liturgical ecclesiology, the church's adoration, proclamation, intercession, and communion do a number of things: mark its obedience to God, build up the faithful, energize serving the needy, signify and testify to God's reign as promise and threat to the world, and much more. But according to von Allmen, a central task of the church at worship is to consecrate *the whole world*. Its purpose is priestly; by its prayer and proclamation, it representatively sanctifies creation, including human beings, space, time, and the cultural products of human effort.

Von Allmen thus closely links the church's representative holiness with its catholicity in his essay *Prophétisme Sacramentel*. There, he writes that one of the central roles of the church in the world is *consécrateur*:

> The Church is not catholic without a precise goal: it is catholic for being holy, for being the place where the things it brings from the world are consecrated, devoted to Jesus Christ. . . . Torn from the profane domain, the 'specimens' of the world are brought back to their true destination, to their true vocation of allies of God. This is why the Church is essentially holy. . . . Jesus Christ sent his Church into the world to claim it and to consecrate it to his

116. von Allmen, *Preaching & Congregation*, 12.
117. von Allmen, *Worship*, 77.

service. Through this consecration, the Church gives people and things their true destination. Everything, in effect, was created not only by Jesus Christ, but for Jesus Christ: he is its head, its leader. Thus, without him, nothing nor anyone in the world is in its rightful place, nothing and no one can fulfill its vocation.[118]

The church fulfills this task by its presence in the world as an eschatological impingement. It foreshadows both the angelic winnowing at the parousia and the universal adoration of Jesus' name at its conclusion. The church's election both distinguishes it from the world and "restores in the Church what the world should be." The world, shriveled up on itself, is surrounded by a shell of autonomy, and it is the church's presence which provides the pressure of the world to come to shatter that shell and provide a "first fruit"—both of what all creation is represented in, and a "first fruit of the shelter in which all of creation can live and survive: a holy nation, a people of priests."[119]

The church, as a people of priests, represents first of all the rest of humanity. Von Allmen cites Barth's *Dogmatics* appreciatively, where he writes: "In the cult, and nowhere else in so direct a manner—the Church's task of provisionally representing the sanctification of humanity in Jesus Christ becomes a really serious concern." In worship, writes von Allmen, in the "freedom that flows from divine forgiveness," human beings become fully themselves, rediscovering their true destiny and vocation.[120]

The church also represents the rest of creation in its worship. The song the world longs to sing is muted now because of the fall, and is perceptible only as a sigh. But in worship, through Christ, who is the head (κεφαλη) of the cosmos, the church brings into worship the "forms, colors, accents, and rhythms" of the world where they are able to "express the truth that the whole earth is full of the Glory of God (Isa 6:3)."[121]

118. von Allmen, *Prophétisme Sacramentel*, 32–33.

119. von Allmen, *Worship*, 32.

120. von Allmen, *Worship*, 72. The representative character of the church in relationship to the rest of humanity has significant implications for the way the church orders itself and its leadership. Yet these implications—particularly those that touch on ordination and ministry—do not hold a central place in von Allmen's *liturgical* writing. We will briefly note what he does say about ordination and order in the appropriate place below. However, at this point, with regard to worship, Von Allmen simply asserts in passing the importance of rejecting a "monopolization of liturgical celebration by the pastor alone."

121. von Allmen, *Worship*, 73. Jean-Jacques von Allmen makes the point here and in several other articles (most notably "A Short Theology of the Place of Worship,") that creation joins human worship, not the other way around: "It is not man who is invited, in

In a similar way, the church makes manifest its holiness, and thus sanctifies the cultural products it makes use of in worship: words, music, and architecture—primary among those von Allmen mentions. Wisely deferring a full discussion of a Christian philosophy of art, von Allmen extends his assertion about creation suggesting that art is "basically the longing of things for liturgical self-expression, to find their justification in the praise for which they were created."[122]

Time and space, too, are sanctified by the church's holy use of them for the purposes of worshipping God. Von Allmen uses the theme of *pars pro toto* and the doctrine of election to argue that the day is sanctified by daily prayer, the week by Sunday worship, and the year by the Easter celebration. "The time given to worship contributes to this sanctification of time . . . because the cult, being celebrated in time, consecrates it and submits it to the Lordship of Christ."[123] In a similar way, a Christian church sanctifies space, identifying the location where Christ might be seen and heard, offering "both a challenge and a promise to other buildings and to space in general."[124]

Liturgical Markers

Our discussion thus far has been primarily theological rather than liturgical. This is entirely in keeping with von Allmen's practice and style. Yet he does make some mention of how the church's holiness is expressed and shaped at particular moments in weekly worship.

For von Allmen, the most important liturgical marker of the church's holiness, as hinted already, is the sacrament of baptism. It is the threshold through which believers cross in order to become part of the new people of God, called to be distinct from the world.[125] It is the sign of ritual purification and forgiveness of sin, as well as a crucial step in the process of salvation.[126] And it is the mystery of the Holy Spirit inspiring and gifting

---

a more or less disguised pantheism, to join in the song of creation, but it is non-human creation which claims its right to worship by joining in that of a regenerated humanity, by making its worship compatible with the latter's" (von Allmen, *Worship*, 73).

122. von Allmen, *Worship*, 109.

123. von Allmen, *Worship*, 237.

124. von Allmen, *Worship*, 282.

125. von Allmen, *Pastorale du Baptême*, II.1.

126. von Allmen, *Pastorale du Baptême*, II.2, II.3, II.5.

for service to God.[127] Although von Allmen devotes an entire chapter of this work to the specifics of liturgical celebration, in it he says very little explicitly about holiness and how the church's holiness is embodied—poorly or well—in this sacrament. However, he does make some connections.

For example, he underscores that baptism is normally public and that it happens on a regular Lord's Day. He also affirms the giving of a new name within the rite, as well as a renunciation along with creedal affirmation. All of these emphasize the holiness of the baptized person and the people as distinct from the world. Similarly, von Allmen discusses one of the preferred locations for the font—at the entrance of the sanctuary—as one that highlights the status of the worshipping people of God as a perfect people: "The church is a holy house in which nothing soiled may enter: one cannot approach the place of God's presence without being regenerated."[128] Likewise, holiness as perfection or purity is also embodied in the ancient practice of clothing the newly baptized in white. He commends Zwingi's post-baptismal prayer: "As you are now bodily clothed in white, may God give you the grace to appear before him, on the last day, with a pure and clean conscience."[129] The baptismal rite—as explained and recommended by von Allmen—also includes two key features that emphasize the church's holiness as a people called to service of God, to ministry. The first is an indirect indicator: the epicletic prayer over the water itself. By it, the water is consecrated to its own liturgical ministry as the water of regeneration. It is not, von Allmen says, made holy in a general or absolute sense but rather made holy specifically "so that it becomes a washing of regeneration for people who repent and accept to recommence their life in Christ."[130] In a parallel way, when someone is baptized and thereby marked as belonging to the Lord, "to serve him all the days of your life" as the prayer cited by von Allmen puts it, the dedicatory aspect of holiness naturally calls for the sign of the cross to be made on the forehead of the newly baptized.[131]

127. von Allmen, *Pastorale du Baptême*, II.4.

128. von Allmen, *Pastorale du Baptême*, II.5.b.

129. At the same time, von Allmen is ambivalent about this practice. Like Zwingli, he thinks clothing in white is symbolically significant, but notes that for that symbolism to work, the one to be baptized must be "entirely unclothed" for baptism, which should ideally take place by immersion. He thinks that public nudity of this sort would cause disruption and complication that make the benefits of its adoption outweighed by its inconveniences. See *Pastorale du Baptême*, IV.6.d.3.

130. von Allmen, *Pastorale du Baptême*, IV.5.c

131. von Allmen, *Pastorale du Baptême*, IV.6.d.6.

In addition to these observations on the sacrament of baptism, von Allmen also points out one other liturgical marker of the church's holiness which is part of every Lord's Day service: prayer. He links prayer to mission as the two primary things the church is called to do in and for the world. The latter is the church's direct calling to proclaim the gospel, the former is her calling to be priests for the world and its needs—and these two reinforce one another. He explains:

> In prayer—whether it consists of praise, repentance, confession or intercession—one brings to Christ-Intercessor all the reasons that one renders grace, adores, repents, confesses, or intercedes. In this sense, prayer prepares mission and results in mission. . . . In its prayer, the Church can draw not only vision from its duty, but also the courage to accomplish it.[132]

These are the only direct references von Allmen makes to the church's holiness in connection with its liturgical celebrations. He makes other more oblique connections, as when he explores the significance of the consecration of gifts and offerings as well as when he speaks of the consecration of the Eucharistic elements in the epicletic prayer.[133] But these have more to do with the sanctification of things put to use by the church than they do with the sanctification of the people themselves.

There are other moments in the Lord's Day liturgy that quite directly connect with the church's holiness—one thinks, for example, of the corporate confession of sin and the assurance of pardon (what von Allmen calls the "humiliation") as a way of making plain the church's renewed holiness. In *Worship*, however, von Allmen's treatment of this liturgical moment is dominated by a discussion of other aspects: history (the lack of such a moment in weekly worship until the eleventh century); the benefits of the *confiteor;* the concern over a "certain automatism" to weekly confession and assurance; and von Allmen's preference for the absolution to be declared in the indicative mood, second-person plural.[134]

---

132. von Allmen, *Prophetisme*, 32.

133. See von Allmen, *Worship*, 295–96; and von Allmen, *Lord's Supper*, 23–36, esp. 30–32.

134. See von Allmen, *Worship*, 290–92. However, in a brief article on "The Forgiveness of Sins as a Sacrament in the Reformed Tradition," von Allmen discusses the relative benefits of corporate and individual aural confession and pardon, noting that a new sense of the "otherness" of the church in a post-Christian culture has resulted in a "deeper awareness of the intrinsic holiness and sanctity of the Church as opposed to the sinfulness of man." His concluding remarks in that article suggest that one key area for

Likewise, one might wish that von Allmen had written more about the church's holiness in connection to the Eucharist. He certainly acknowledges that the Supper energizes mission and service, that the meal is the impingement on the present of the eschatological (which has implications for the church's holiness), etc. Yet it was never von Allmen's intention to construct a comprehensive liturgical ecclesiology.

Summary

Jean-Jacques von Allmen identifies a number of aspects of ecclesial holiness in his writings on preaching, worship, and the sacraments. Among them are holiness as distinction, perfection, dedication, and representation. We have explored a few liturgical markers that von Allmen identifies as connected to ecclesial holiness, noting that his work here is thinner than we might like. Theologically speaking, it is also rather straightforward. One might wish for a richer treatment that explored holiness through the paradox of the "just sinner," or the people in—but not of—the world. Von Allmen used such dialectical pairings throughout his treatment of the Lord's Supper, and Gordon Lathrop's treatment of holiness shows how it might be done fruitfully:

> The Christian practice of holiness must always involve the subversion of all religious ideas of holiness. If Jesus Christ is our holiness, then holiness is no longer separation and ritual purity and perfect observance . . . it is connection with others. It is the unclear cross and life through death and welcome to the outsiders and transformative mercy for the world.[135]

CATHOLICITY

St. Ignatius is the first of the church Fathers, early in the second century, to use the adjective *catholic* to describe the church. "Wherever Jesus Christ is, there is the catholic church."[136] Twenty centuries later, in *Doxology,*

---

theologians to work on is to address the question "What is the relationship of confession as a community (as a church) to the belief in the holiness of the Church?" Yet he does not travel that interesting path in that article nor in any other that I am aware of. See von Allmen, "Forgiveness of Sins," 112–19.

135. Lathrop, *Holy People*, 211. See also Lathrop, *Holy Things*, 132–38.

136. Ignatius quoted in Stone, *Reader*, 14. Ignatius makes this assertion in a

Geoffrey Wainwright takes his cue from St. Ignatius: he begins his discussion of the catholicity of the church by pointing to Jesus. The church is the body of Christ, and what is true of Christ is true of the church. The Bible's soteriological claim is that Christ's work on the cross and his vindication and resurrection will ultimately draw all people and all things to himself.[137] The Bible's Christological claim is that God has given Jesus a name above all names, and one day every knee shall bend and every tongue offer him worship.[138] Thus, says Wainwright, the "implied vocation of the Church is to catholicity."[139]

The term's primary reference, of course, is not solely to the Roman Catholic Church, as Protestant catechetical materials are quick to point out.[140] Likewise, its meaning is something richer than a simple universality. Indeed, the Greek etymology suggests wholeness and integrity as well as inclusivity and comprehensiveness.[141] Ecclesiologists often distinguish, then, between two basic aspects of what it means for the church to be catholic. It is catholic in geographical universality; i.e., it is worldwide, even cosmic, in its scope. Further, it is catholic in conceptual universality; i.e., it encompasses all of human experience and conditions, despite cultural factors that might otherwise cause division and enmity.[142]

Jean-Jacques von Allmen's treatment of ecclesial catholicity is a bit more expansive. The term, he writes, is "one of the finest and richest in Christian ecclesiology."[143] He names and explores not two, but five as-

---

subordinate clause as he makes an argument for the exclusive validity of communities and worship sanctioned by a duly ordained bishop. This quote is, therefore, not a particularly good place to look for affirmation of the present variety of church communities and inter-ecclesial recognition, which is the direction toward which many conversations about catholicity tend to push.

137. See Eph 1:10; John 12:32; etc.

138. See Phil 2:10–22; Rev 5:13–14; etc.

139. Wainwright, *Doxology*, 133.

140. See, for example, "Second Helvetic Confession," chapter XVII: "We, therefore, call this Church catholic because it is universal, scattered through all parts of the world, and extended unto all times, and is not limited to any times or places. Therefore, we condemn the Donatists who confined the Church to I know not what corners of Africa. Nor do we approve of the Roman clergy who have recently passed off only the Roman Church as catholic."

141. See Meyendorff, "Orthodox Concept of the Church," 61.

142. See, for example, Thomas Aquinas's, "Exposition on the Apostles' Creed," quoted in Stone, *Reader*, 67.

143. von Allmen, *Worship*, 69.

pects of this identifying mark of the church: sociological, anthropological, spatial, temporal, and liturgical. Furthermore, he makes connections
between this and other Nicene marks, such as holiness and unity. However,
his treatment of catholicity in his liturgical writings (our primary focus)
explicitly eschews tackling the problem most ecclesiologists find central to
this topic: the relationship between the local church and the church which
transcends them and in which they participate. What follows, then, will
divide our discussion into five brief sections, treating each of the aspects
of catholicity von Allmen identifies in turn. This will be followed by a section on liturgical markers of catholicity and then some summary remarks
on the relationship between the local church, the catholic church, and the
liturgical expression of the same.

Sociological catholicity

For von Allmen, the church's baptismal identity means that it is fundamentally opposed to anything that divides and separates. Of course, baptism
itself is the mark of a kind of division and separation—of the sacred from
the profane, a welcoming and gathering "all for whom Jesus Christ died,
all who in him are destined for salvation."[144] But beyond this separation,
the church's catholicity means that it stands beyond and against common
sociological and cultural barriers. It is a welcoming place for all people, rich
or poor, powerful or weak, foolish or clever, Jew or Greek, slave or free, man
or woman. In the church, writes von Allmen, there is "no room for pride,
covetousness, exploitation, and envy. Where the world separates or con-
fuses, the Church distinguishes and unites."[145] This feature of the church's
catholicity, at least at the congregational level, is aspirational more than
actual, and has significant liturgical implications, seen below.

Anthropological catholicity

In the same way that the church's catholicity is a sign of its welcome for
society in its fullness, it is also a sign of its welcome for humanity in its
fullness. Salvation extends to, and life in Christ within the church embraces, the whole range of human thought, feeling, willing, and activity. Von

144. von Allmen, *Worship*, 50.
145. von Allmen, *Worship*, 48.

Allmen points to Jesus' healing miracles as paradigmatic proclamations of this restored humanity, and notes the range of human faculties healed—not just eyes or ears, but lips, limbs, minds, and hearts: "Jesus did not cure only the deaf, and the breadth of His healing miracles has evident liturgical implications."[146] Interestingly, von Allmen does not articulate precisely what those "evident" liturgical implications are—but one may surmise that he means to suggest that at worship, the Triune God meets his people not merely that they can hear God speak to them, but that their whole selves, in fullness and fellowship, may come to pray, praise, and petition, to weep and dance and sing, to speak and listen and eat and wash and love.

Spatial catholicity

Human beings are divided by cultural forces and social attributes. They are divided within themselves and they are divided geographically, scattered in the countryside or clumped in urban areas, associated with one political entity or another. The church's spatial catholicity repudiates what von Allmen calls the "indifferent or bellicose juxtapositions of cities and nations."[147] One may participate in a local congregation or even an affiliation of congregations with national connections (i.e., the Dutch Reformed Church or the Church of England), yet the church's catholicity transcends them all. Jean-Jacques von Allmen points to the "injunctions and examples reported in the New Testament of intercessions and thanksgiving by distant churches" as a way of seeing what this sort of catholicity means in practice. The conclusion to this section will return to the notion of shared gifts among churches as a way of marking catholicity in the church's worshipping practices.

This "horizontal" spatial dimension is augmented, according to von Allmen, by what he calls a "vertical" dimension, to "heaven and the abode of the dead"—though 'spiritual' dimension might be more appropriate. By this he means the supernatural participation in worship of angels, who are "partners in worship."[148] In fact, von Allmen has a rather significant section on the participation of the angels in the cult in a section in *Worship* on the "participants in the cult." After some preliminary remarks about what sort of beings they are (marginal, with the ability to surround and obey), von

146. von Allmen, *Worship*, 49.

147. von Allmen, *Worship*, 48.

148. von Allmen, *Worship*, 49.

Allmen quotes Peter Brunner and Karl Barth at length, speaking of worship of the church as a "pale and broken reflection of what takes place in heaven." But more than earthly worship joining the heavenly—at moments such as the *trisagion* in the Great Prayer of Thanksgiving—the angels join their worship to ours in a number of ways and at various moments. The book of Revelation, von Allmen points out, has a special guardian angel for each church, commissioned to guard and to guide it. Liturgical duties that may fall to angels, he speculates, are the presentation of our prayers to the Father (see Rev 5:8; 8:3), the profession of faith, doxological acclamations, and especially preaching, as the New Testament witness has angels present when the great works of God are proclaimed (e.g., the nativity, the resurrection, the ascension, etc.).[149]

Temporal catholicity

When the church gathers to worship, Christ is present, and where Christ is present, "all those whom He has saved are present also."[150] Thus, the catholicity of the church has a temporal dimension as well, as the church at worship welcomes the faith, testimony, and presence of all the elect from the past—and the future. As von Allmen describes it:

> In its worship, the Church bears witness that it unites the centuries, refusing to allow what is past to fall into oblivion, or what is promised to fade into illusion. It is, as St. Bernard used to say, *ante et retro oculata*, it sees before and behind, and embraces the totality of the process of salvation. When in worship, the Church emerges as what it is, the whole history of salvation is secretly present from Abel to the parousia.[151]

Liturgical catholicity

The aspects of catholicity discussed up to this point are important variations on a familiar theme for ecclesiologists. But von Allmen adds a last aspect of ecclesial catholicity, connected to his thoughts on "representative

149. von Allmen, *Worship*, 205–9.
150. von Allmen, *Worship*, 198.
151. von Allmen, *Worship*, 49.

holiness,"[152] that is a bit unusual. The church, says von Allmen, is catholic in the same way that Noah's Ark was. That is to say, the church is a "guarantor"[153] of the world, a bearer of the world's future. In its worship, it collects and gathers the "sighs and longings" of all creation and restores them to their liturgical vocation.[154] This is the same theme that von Allmen develops more fully in the essay *Prophétisme Sacramentel*: "Claiming, in the name of the Lord, the entire world, the church must reach all the elements of the present century to bring back 'specimens.' This is why the Church is essentially catholic."[155] The church fulfills this function through its prayer (as discussed above) and in mission, understood not primarily as the "expansion of Christianity through space and time" but rather a re-assembly of parts that have been scattered. The comparison to Noah's Ark is extended by von Allmen as he compares the church to a zoo:

> Will one pardon an example which is not very theological, but which permits a good understanding of what we are hearing? Just as the management of a zoological garden finances expeditions which capture several animal specimens that it is lacking, in the same way Jesus Christ sends his Church into the world so that the world will be found complete in the Church. . . . The "specimens" of the world reached by the church are captured by it, and the Church makes them captives of Christ, and they are added to the Church only after having renounced themselves, after dying to their autonomy: the Church baptizes them. This captivity does not level them nor allow them to be merged: baptism does not interrupt their identity but, on the contrary, fulfills it completely, and they become themselves—in the fullest sense of the term—by finding their true vocation because they are possessed by Christ. A baptized Swede cannot be merged, because he is integrated into the Church, with a baptized Sinhalese, who also cannot be merged, because they are both enclosed in a zoological garden, like an elephant and a platypus![156]

152. This highlights the ways in which there are areas of overlap when we speak of the marks of the church—how ecclesial unity and holiness and catholicity intersect. So, for example, in a single sentence, von Allmen can connect these three: "If true worship is holy because it brings the baptized before the Saviour, it is catholic because it unites, before the Lord, the completed number of the elect" (von Allmen, *Worship*, 199).

153. Fr. *revendicateur*

154. von Allmen, *Worship*, 50.

155. von Allmen, *Prophétisme*, 26.

156. von Allmen, *Prophétisme*, 28–29. I suspect that von Allmen's fondness for zoos

Liturgical Markers

Our review of von Allmen's discussion of angels showed how he linked the church's catholicity to its worship. But a more thorough exploration of the liturgical markers of ecclesial catholicity has been deferred up to this point. Because von Allmen is not intentionally constructing a liturgical ecclesiology, he does not note these liturgical markers in a systematic way. Even so, we will try to present them as fully as the material allows us to do so.

Ordo. The first sign of the church's catholicity expressed liturgically is its worshipping order. For von Allmen, the fundamental shape of Lord's Day worship is the two-fold rhythm of apostolic witness (i.e., preaching) and Communion; the mass of the catechumens and the mass of the faithful. He does not construct a careful argument for this *ordo* as normative for the universal church, which would involve a careful marshaling of biblical and historical sources, etc. But he does assert that this rhythm was the normative pattern for the first fifteen centuries of the church's life until the reformation.[157] Its widespread and consistent use in those centuries make it one of the key features of worship that is truly catholic: "We have not the right, unless we wish to injure the catholicity of our confession, to regard the Eucharist as an optional rather than an essential element in the cult."[158]

Preaching. The second sign of the church's catholicity as it finds liturgical expression is in the proclamation of the Word, especially in the preaching moment. Preaching expresses temporal catholicity, connecting the history of salvation to the present moment. It "reminds the Church of all places and times of the vocation which God proposes for her here and now."[159] Preaching also speaks to the universality of the Word of God—a Word expressed in the fleshly particularity of language, yet the preexistent logos by which the world was created. Preaching also moves between the universal and the particular in that the reconciliation of the whole world was accomplished through particular historical events, the story of the

---

blinded him to the significant negative implications of this metaphor. If the church is like a zoo, how does the captivity of a creature in a cage square with von Allmen's language of the world and its specimens becoming what they were meant to be and finding their true vocation in church? In what way does a platypus or elephant realize its true vocation and purpose in captivity in a zoo (even if the captivity is relatively benevolent)?

157. von Allmen, *Worship*, 284.

158. von Allmen, *Worship*, 288.

159. von Allmen, *Preaching & Congregation*, 36.

birth, ministry, passion, victory, and glory of Jesus the Jew, from Nazareth in Palestine:

> The universal is valid only in the particular forms which it assumes and in which it conceals itself; indeed we have no direct access to it. It is only through mediation, through particular examples, that we can reach it. God is the God of our fathers, the God of Abraham, of Isaac and of Jacob, and not the God of the philosophers.[160]

The Lord's Supper. Another liturgical marker of the church's catholicity is her celebration of the Lord's Supper. This is most apparent in von Allmen's insistence upon the meal as a regular and normative feature of the church's weekly worship, in unity with the majority of Christian congregations in her first fifteen centuries. In fact, von Allmen does not speak with much clarity and distinctiveness about the ways in which the Eucharist expresses temporal, spatial, anthropological, or sociological catholicity. He does make connections to other marks of the church—unity and holiness—that overlap with his discussions on catholicity. For example, in his conversation about the nearly universal celebration of the Lord's Supper in the churches, he says that diversity, in its celebration among all the churches, did not compromise its unity.[161] In fact, the unique character of each congregation's celebration, its localization in the celebration of a transcendent rite, gives proof of its catholicity[162]: "the celebration of the Supper fully establishes the congregation which celebrates as a church; it identifies the congregation as a messianic people celebrating the history of salvation and therefore integrated into this history by its very Eucharistic celebration."[163] The meal as an eschatological event also makes each local congregation aware of the eschatological nature of the whole church, aware of the "inter-and transnational" solidarity she shares.[164]

But the Lord's Supper especially underscores what von Allmen calls its liturgical catholicity—a notion closely connected with his notion of representative holiness. In this, the use of 'specimens' of the world—specifically, bread and wine—is a way in which the meal gathers up all of creation to participate in the feast:

160. von Allmen, *Preaching & Congregation*, 21–22.
161. von Allmen, *Worship*, 15.
162. von Allmen, *Lord's Supper*, 37.
163. von Allmen, *Lord's Supper*, 47.
164. von Allmen, *Lord's Supper*, 40.

The Eucharistic gathering is "kat'holique" in the full sense of the term because it represents Christ and the members of Christ gathered from all places and ages, because it embodies all the gifts of grace. But this catholicity is too exuberant, too joyful, too vital, to be confined within these bounds, so that it becomes a promise and an opportunity for the whole world, men, and things, even if they do not yet believe in this promise or grasp this opportunity. . . . At the moment of the Eucharist, creation finds access again to real worship, recovers her primary orientation, which is doxological.[165]

Baptism. Baptism, too, is a liturgical marker of ecclesial catholicity, though von Allmen does not go into much detail in his discussion of this point. He notes that baptism joins to the church in two senses: "it joins [the baptized] to the 'catholic' church, to the church according to its fullness, to the body of Christ, to the people who attest to the mystery of salvation."[166] It also joins to the local church: "Tradition is practically unanimous on this point: to be part of the church, it is necessary to belong to a congregation."[167] This is reflected in the baptismal rite, in whatever specific words may be used, in a greeting and welcome, which are offered by a specific congregation on behalf of the catholic church.

Worship. In addition to these and other previously mentioned liturgical moments, von Allmen makes particular note of the church's use of common prayers and confessions of faith as expressions of its catholicity. In connection with these remarks, he grinds a bit of his own axe when he insists, "If the liturgy attaches the church of here and now to the Church of all places and all times, if it adores God's faithfulness, we shall best respect it by . . . [refusing] to modify liturgical texts accepted by the Church and demonstrated by her to be in accordance with the scriptural canon. In particular we must now make the Lord's prayer into a theme with variations."[168]

Summary and Critique

Von Allmen identifies five aspects of ecclesial catholicity: sociological, anthropological, spatial, temporal, and liturgical. For von Allmen, the catholicity of the church can be demonstrated in the sacraments, preaching, and

165. von Allmen, *Lord's Supper*, 49.
166. von Allmen, *Pastorale du Baptême*, II.1.b
167. von Allmen, *Pastorale du Baptême*, II.1.b.
168. von Allmen, *Preaching & Congregation*, 37.

a handful of liturgical moments. Yet the central, defining issue of ecclesial catholicity for many ecclesiologists has remained unexamined so far: the relationship between local congregations and the universal, transcendent church. The topic is complex. Is the church a composite made up of many constituent churches? If so, is each congregation fully a church, or does each have a diminished or franchised ecclesiality? Is the only true complete church a local congregation, and notions of anything more exalted or transcendent merely platonic abstractions rather than spiritual realities? If the church is present wherever Christ is present (as Ignatius wrote), then what is the role of the Eucharist in making Christ present that an assembly may be "church"? Does the Holy Spirit have a role? Does every local congregation have equal standing with every other congregation, or are some churches more "church" than others? Do local assemblies exist as church—as the body of Christ—independent of other assemblies, or are they dependent? And if the latter, in what way? Does it matter whether and how one congregation recognizes another congregation as a "church"?

One can see that there is rich area of inquiry related to ecclesial catholicity. But we have deferred addressing this aspect of the topic until now because von Allmen explicitly eschews it, asserting that it is tangential and perhaps too unwieldy to tackle when worship is the primary focus:

> In particular, to avoid having to introduce into this treatise on liturgy a whole treatise on ecclesiology, we must pass over the problem of the relations between the local Church (i.e. the liturgical assembly) and the universal Church, and that of the catholic authorization of the normal ministry of the local Church, of the liturgical PROISTAMENOS (Rom 12: 8; 1 Thess 5:12).[169]

It is not that these issues are unimportant to von Allmen, or that he does not address them. He does.[170] Yet when he does, it is from a purely

169. von Allmen, *Worship*, 52.

170. See, for example, the essays, "La continuite de l'Eglise salon la doctrine réformée" and "Loyauté confessional et violent œcuménique" in *Prophétisme Sacramentel*, as well as the second chapter of *Une réforme dans l'Eglise*.

His most substantive treatment is in an article, "L'Église locale parmi les autres églises locale," written just before his departure for the Tantur Institute in Jerusalem. In it, he calls for an ecclesiological debate on how a local church must be church among the other local churches. That debate should proceed, he argues, from three starting points: first, that a local church must not only claim catholicity for itself; it must be recognized as part of the church by other local congregations. And in fact, he says, a local assembly's request to be so acknowledged is its own way of acknowledging the others as church themselves. Second, he argues that the "mutual recognition of the constitutive ecclesiality of churches

theological and not liturgical point of view (albeit with a rich biblical basis). That is to say, even when he explores this issue in depth elsewhere, he makes no note of any implications for the worshipping assembly. By his own criteria, then, this aspect of ecclesial catholicity might be seen as relatively unimportant.[171] However, another liturgical theologian, Gordon Lathrop, following in von Allmen's footsteps and starting from his premise (worship as the epiphany of the church), demonstrates how in fact these ecclesial issues *do* have liturgical implications.

In the second chapter of *Holy People*, Lathrop speaks of the connection, the *communion* each local assembly has with every other:

> Because of God's presence,[172] our local meeting becomes the whole catholic church dwelling here. . . . Because of God's acting, not because of our intuiting the universal in the particular, each local meeting becomes a sign of the dawning of the day of God.[173]

But Lathrop goes on to speak of the *signs* of this communion and mutuality between local congregations, not in ecclesial structures (where von Allmen focuses), but in the assembly at worship:

> The linkage between local and more-than-local, between the assembly of God in this city and the whole catholic assembly in all the inhabited earth, is neither mystical nor hierarchical nor merely organizational nor invisible. It is theological and concretely liturgical.[174]

Going where von Allmen pointed but did not tread, Lathrop recalls the New Testament witness to mutual gift-giving among local congregations as a model for a *liturgical* expression of catholicity. In a substantive list, he names the canon of scripture and lectionary lists themselves as one such gift from local congregations from long ago, as well as patterns and examples of preaching, baptism, intercession, and daily prayer—"fragments from their patterns of liturgical life." He points to the shape of the Lord's Day *ordo* and

---

requires a structure." Finally, he argues that previous proposals to describe and operate this unitive structure have never been satisfactory to all churches. Collegiate models are repugnant to the Roman church and primatial models are repugnant to Protestants. See von Allmen, "L'Église locale parmi," 512–37.

171. Recall von Allmen's claim that theological questions without liturgical implications are of secondary importance to the church.

172. In the risen Christ and in the outpoured Spirit.

173. Lathrop, *Holy People*, 53.

174. Lathrop, *Holy People*, 54.

to practices of Eucharistic celebration, to creeds and catechisms used in worship, and to "songs, hymns, and other music," among many other gifts congregations can give and have given to one another.[175] Among many congregations and congregational leaders, this sort of sharing is very common today, especially the sharing of music and other artistic resources—made easier by technology for printing and electronic distribution.

Von Allmen certainly affirmed the need for liturgical enculturation, for every congregation to worship in its own particular way, in the "*hic et nunc* of its pilgrimage," while still being subject to certain transcendent norms.[176] Across the church's catholic vastness, there is a "deep unity" but not uniformity. He writes: "A cult in Madagascar can legitimately be expressed differently from a cult in Scandanavia," and extending from geographical to temporal catholicity, he says: "a cult of the twentieth century can find other forms of expression from those of a cult in the third or the eleventh centuries."[177] And von Allmen was certainly aware of ways in which various congregations and church cultures could share liturgical resources such as music. His affection for African-American spirituals (which he called "Jordanian melodies") has already been noted. Though few theologians were addressing this explicitly before Vatican II, one wishes that von Allmen had explored the relationship between ecclesial catholicity and liturgical enculturation in more depth. When congregations develop their own indigenous worship practices, nurturing their own musicians and other artists, they become more deeply aware of their identity as a local catholic church. When they share their gifts and make use of the gifts from other churches, shared both synchronically and diachronically, they become more deeply aware of their communion with the church in all its broad catholicity.[178]

175. Lathrop, *Holy People*, 57–58.

176. See von Allmen, *Worship*, 96. He identifies these norms as deriving from the New Testament.

177. von Allmen, *Worship*, 100.

178. Consider, for instance, the Nairobi Statement on Worship and Culture, released in 1996 by the Lutheran World Federation, and which Lathrop had a hand in developing. Excerpted in an appendix in *Holy People*, the statement speaks of a kind of artistic catholicity: "The sharing of hymns and art and other elements of worship across cultural barriers helps enrich the whole church and strengthen the sense of the *communio* of the church" (Lathrop, *Holy People*, 236).

APOSTOLICITY

According to the book of Ephesians, the household of God is "built upon the foundation of the apostles and prophets" (Eph 2:20). Christ is the cornerstone, and the church that is genuinely faithful to the life, witness, and mission given first-hand by Jesus to the apostles, is authentically apostolic. But the meaning and significance of this mark of the church is problematic, especially in its use discerning a true church from a false one—owing in part to the continuing disputes over apostolic succession, the shape of the episcopate, and the primacy of the Bishop of Rome.[179]

In many ways, this mark stands apart from the other three. Unity, holiness, and catholicity connect and overlap in various ways, yet apostolicity is the ground of them all. Karl Barth writes that the fourth mark "does not simply stand in a row with the other three expressions, but explains them."[180] That is to say, the church that is one, holy, and catholic *is* apostolic. The difficulty lies in testing apostolic authenticity—discerning whether and to what extent a church rests on that foundation. Are its leaders authorized to do what they do by the apostles? Does it retain and transmit the salient truth of the apostolic message? Is the community faithful to the apostolic mission, its work in the world? These questions outline three basic approaches to apostolicity, approaches that naturally reflect the ecclesiological positions of those who hold them. Roman Catholics classically emphasize the continuity of the messengers. Protestants classically emphasize the continuity of the message itself. And more recently, influenced by free-church communities, others emphasize the continuity of messaging—the ecclesial characteristic of being a sent people, living up to the "apostolic life of commitment and evangelization."[181]

Our survey of Jean-Jacques von Allmen's writings about liturgy—the four books on worship, preaching, the Lord's Supper, and baptism that have been our focus—has revealed that while he does not explicitly distinguish

179. Apostolic succession and its relationship to Roman claims of primacy is certainly an important topic in any treatment of ecclesial apostolicity. However, it does not seem central to this project—i.e., a liturgical ecclesiology. It receives very little attention in the four primary volumes by von Allmen under consideration here. However, it is important for ongoing ecumenical conversations, and von Allmen certainly addresses the topic in detail in other places. See von Allmen, "Les Conditions d'une intercommunion acceptable," 13–20; "Ordination: A Sacrament?" 40–48; "Continuity of the Church," 424–44; and especially his larger work, *La Primauté de l'Eglise*.

180. Barth, *Dogmatics in Outline*, 147.

181. Kärkäinen, *Introduction*, 75.

between these basic aspects of ecclesial apostolicity, he also does not fall neatly into the expected "Protestant" camp, emphasizing only one type. He uses "apostolic" and related terms in at least four ways:

- *Foundational* apostolicity—to describe the practice and theology of the very earliest church traditions, the testimony of the eyewitnesses to Christ's life, death, and resurrection.[182]

- *Institutional* apostolicity—to describe the safeguarding of the witness, mission, and authority of the apostles through their successors via the episcopate, signified by the laying on of hands.[183]

- *Theological* apostolicity—to describe the faithful transmission of doctrine and practice (word and sacrament), the distillation or expansion of the gospel message originally given to the apostles in and by Jesus.

- *Missional* apostolicity—to describe the faithful activity of the church in its primary vocation to join God's mission in the world, as a people sent to announce, point to, and manifest the reign of God.

What follows, then, is an examination of what von Allmen has to say about each of these aspects of apostolicity. This will be followed by a look at the liturgical markers for each, recognizing that in some ways, apostolicity is the *least* manifest in worship.

Then we will offer some summary remarks on missional apostolicity. It is here that we fold in a discussion that might be expanded elsewhere, exploring the church's *activities* as well as its identity. We lament the thin attention given in von Allmen's writing to the church's activities that take place outside of the sphere of worship, and we point out this area as one where further work would be helpful.

Foundational

J.-J. von Allmen uses the term apostolic in a foundational sense to describe the character, practice, or theology of the very earliest church traditions. He writes of the Corinthian church being characterized by a "charismatic

---

182. This will include a type of *liturgical* apostolicity—to describe specifically the worship practices of the very earliest church traditions—used only in the broadest way, as detailed historical certainty about apostolic worship practices is quite thin.

183. Avery Dulles calls this *juridical* apostolicity. Others call it mechanical or historical. In any case, it fundamentally has to do with church polity.

effervescence"[184] and the apostolic church (in general) living in the "expectation of an imminent parousia."[185] He notes that those who ate and drank with Christ after his resurrection had an "apostolic consciousness" of themselves as witnesses to remarkable events.[186] He refers to apostolic liturgical practices, such as the reading of scripture,[187] the kiss of peace,[188] the gathering on Sunday,[189] facing East to pray,[190] the use of wine at the Lord's Supper,[191] or a greeting in the Lord's name, such as those that begin Pauline epistles.[192] The practice of paedobaptism is also called apostolic, as von Allmen relies on Origen's assertion that "the Church received the tradition to baptize also young children from the apostles."[193] More significantly, he notes that Jesus commanded that the apostles celebrate the Lord's Supper,[194] though he recognizes that given the differences between the accounts in Paul and the synoptics, it is appropriate to have some suspicion about discerning with historical certainly the "apostolic" manner of celebrating the Lord's Supper.[195] He also asserts that the "apostolic witness" testifies to the real presence of Christ in the Lord's Supper.[196] And finally, he notes that the early church devoted itself to the "teaching of the apostles," as noted in Acts 2. In nearly all these cases, he bases his sense of what is foundationally apostolic on a text from scripture, our primary record of what the Apostles said and did. In sum, von Allmen articulates a very basic sense of what apostolic means in this way: "The true Church is that of the *apostles:* to be Christian, one has to be member of a Church affiliated with the apostolic Church . . . because the authentic bearers of the Spirit are the apostles, the indubitable witnesses of the new eschatology that appeared

---

184. von Allmen, *Worship*, 190.

185. von Allmen, *Worship*, 228.

186. von Allmen, *Lord's Supper*, 56.

187. von Allmen, *Worship*, 131.

188. von Allmen, *Worship*, 174–75.

189. von Allmen, *Worship*, 222.

190. von Allmen, *Worship*, 226.

191. von Allmen, *Worship*, 246.

192. von Allmen, *Worship*, 138.

193. von Allmen, *Pastorale du Baptême*, III.2.b

194. von Allmen, *The Lord's Supper*, 46.

195. von Allmen, *The Lord's Supper*, 10–12.

196. von Allmen, *The Lord's Supper*, 56.

with Christ's resurrection, those who give assurance that one's faith is not an illusion—they are the apostles."[197]

Institutional

Avery Dulles writes that in Roman Catholic apologetics from the fifteenth through the twentieth centuries, apostolicity was understood through the lens of institutional ecclesiology. The Roman Church maintained fidelity to the character, theology, and practice of the apostles through government or office, "for the office had the power to declare what were true doctrines and true sacraments. Apostolicity therefore meant for these apologists the legitimate succession of pastors, and the approval of the pastors was seen as coming from Rome."[198] We see here the basic elements of an institutional understanding of apostolicity. For a Protestant in the Reformed tradition, von Allmen has surprising sympathy with the aspects of apostolicity that express how the apostolicity of the church is safeguarded through the institutional authorization of a particular individual. He writes, for example, that the One who presides at the table in Christian worship needs to be someone "authorized by Christ, acknowledged by congregation as Christ's envoy and recognized by other local churches as worthy and able and authorized to do so."[199] Elsewhere, in the context of speaking about the participants in worship, he notes that the head of the worshipping community has a "threefold ministry." First, the leader is the "commissioned representative of the Lord and in consequence the successor of the apostles. What he does he does in the name of and with the authority of his master. His presence at the head of worship is one of the signs of the real presence of Christ among his own."[200] Second, according to von Allmen, the worship leader "ensures the valid Christian character of worship." Here, he cites the Second Helvetic Confession that the true church is found where the gospel is rightly proclaimed and the sacraments administered "by legitimately appointed pastors."[201] Finally, von Allmen says that the third aspect of the ministry of the worship leader is to "ensure that all is done which ought to

197. von Allmen, *Pastorale Baptême*, II.4.b

198. Dulles, *Models of the Church*, 129.

199. von Allmen, *The Lord's Supper*, 46.

200. von Allmen, *Worship*, 192.

201. von Allmen, *Worship*, 192. Of course, this raises the question of what it means to be "legitimately appointed."

be done" in worship.[202] This section reveals not an emphasis on authorization of the successors to the apostles by physical laying on of hands; rather, the apostolicity of the meeting and the people is guaranteed in part at least by the ministry of the *person* who simply does these things.

In line with his ecumenical sensibilities, von Allmen, however, does indeed have sympathy with the notion—more typically associated with Roman, Orthodox, and Anglican traditions—that churches need to be connected, through an ordained priest, to a church founded by an apostle, normally by the laying on of hands. He assesses the Pauline dispute with the Jerusalem church recorded in Acts as one not of doctrine, but of Paul's legal, institutional right to found churches. For if Paul is not an apostle, the churches he has founded are not real churches. Von Allmen rehearses this argument in a number of places.[203] In his 1982 farewell lecture to the University of Neuchâtel (a document examined more closely in the next section), he writes:

> The Church is a local Christian congregation founded by an apostle or his claim settled within the church by an apostle. . . . The Church is apostolic because it is not only sent worldwide to make known the resurrection of Jesus. The Church is apostolic by the fact that she is personally bound to an apostle, and thus empowered by the legitimate Risen One himself to convey those who accept the gospel "from the power of darkness into the kingdom of the beloved Son of God in whom we have redemption, the forgiveness of sins" (Col 1:13).[204]

Interestingly, for von Allmen—and here he demonstrates his Protestant inclinations—apostolic succession itself is less about what Dulles calls juridical authorization or the properly sanctioned presidency of the sacraments, and more about the ministry of the Word. In *Preaching and Congregation*, he argues that, historically, the criterion of apostolic succession was faithfulness to the apostolic witness—obedient transmission of

202. At this point, von Allmen lists his sense of those things: the worship leader sets the time and place of worship, summons the congregation, greets in the name of the Lord, announces the Word of God in clerical and prophetic proclamation, celebrates Holy Communion and supervises its administration, recites some of the prayers (as mouthpiece of people), consecrates the people's offering, and dismisses the people with God's blessing. See von Allmen, *Worship*, 192.

203. These places include von Allmen, *Lord's Supper*, 51, and von Allmen, *Pastorale du Baptême*, III.3.b, among others.

204. von Allmen, "Les marques de l'Eglise," 97–107.

the apostolic tradition. This became a crucial problem at the reformation *not*, he says, because of the claim implicit in Roman apostolic succession to "safeguard the historical character of the life of the church," but because "those who claim to be part of this succession failed to transmit the apostolic witness simply and faithfully, and have since been unwilling either to recognize or repent of this fact."[205] The particularly Reformed contribution to ecumenical conversation, he writes, can be offered at precisely this point: first of all, to trust the "historical character of grace" and thus accept the idea and term "succession," and then to insist that it be tied not to the valid celebration of the sacraments, but to faithfulness "in translating and making present the apostolic witness."[206] In this von Allmen clearly points in the direction we look to next: theological apostolicity.

Theological

The complaint of the reformers—and von Allmen's complaint, too—is that apostolic succession through institutional mechanisms does not necessarily guarantee that the doctrine and practice of the apostles will indeed be transmitted faithfully. Under such circumstances, the church can be confident that the gospel will continue to be proclaimed if apostolicity is understood in the sense of "continuity with the faith and the proclamation of the apostles. The sacraments and ecclesiastical office are subordinated to the preaching of the gospel."[207] This same aspect of apostolicity is articulated in von Allmen with regard to the importance of reading scripture in worship. He speaks of the miracle of preaching, that by the power of the Holy Spirit, the Word "comes alive for us so as to accomplish its work of salvation and judgment."[208] Yet if preaching could do this alone, he argues, the apostles could have easily relied solely on oral tradition. But "the very fact that they buried their witness to Jesus Christ in these hieroglyphic signs that are letters proves that they believed the Spirit-inspired interpretation of these hieroglyphs would be able to resurrect their witness and enable themselves to remain alive in the Church."[209]

---

205. von Allmen, *Preaching & Congregation*, 63.

206. von Allmen, *Preaching & Congregation*, 63.

207. Dulles, *Models of the Church*, 139.

208. von Allmen, *Worship*, 133.

209. von Allmen, *Worship*, 133.

And what is at the heart of this witness? For von Allmen, the answer is Jesus. He is very Barthian in his understanding of the relationship between preaching, Scripture, and Jesus—between the proclaimed word of God, the written Word of God, and the pre-existent Word who became flesh in the man from Galilee.[210] "The text of the Word which we have to translate and make present is preserved in Holy Scripture, the canonical witness of the apostles," writes von Allmen in *Preaching & Congregation*. And what scripture does is provide us with reliable testimony—from the apostles and prophets—about Jesus. "Our preaching will be faithful not in proportion to its apparent adherence to a biblical text, but in the measure in which it understands and communicates that text as a direct or indirect witness to the action which God undertook in and for the world through His Son."[211]

More than this, for von Allmen, ecclesial apostolicity is tied not merely to the gospel accounts of Jesus' life, death, and resurrection but also to theological statements about these events and their meaning. Writing about baptism as an eschatological judgment, he says that he cannot summarize, for "it would be necessary to cite the entire New Testament." Yet he has a go, writing: "By being condemned and executed, Jesus brought on himself God's last judgment against a rebellious people. God thus demonstrated that he *wanted* to end man's misery, and by raising Jesus from the dead, he demonstrated that he *could* end their misery."[212] One might certainly dispute whether this articulation is indeed the heart of the apostolic witness, but the point here is that, for von Allmen, the apostolic witness is understood to be not only the facts about Jesus' life and death but also a particular doctrinal understanding of their meaning.

At the same time, von Allmen recognizes the creeds as especially significant summaries of the apostolic faith. When he commends their regular use in weekly worship during the "confession of faith," he remarks that this

210. Consider, for example, Barth's doctrine of the Word of God, where the Word of God has three modes of existence: The Word incarnate (Revelation), the Word written (Holy Scripture), and the Word proclaimed in preaching: "It is one and the same whether we understand [the Word of God] as revelation, Bible, or proclamation. There is no distinction of degree or value between the three forms. . . . The revealed Word of God we know only from Scripture adopted by church proclamation or the proclamation of the church based on Scripture. The written Word of God we know only through the revelation that fulfills proclamation or through the proclamation fulfilled by revelation. The preached Word of God we know only through the revelation attested in Scripture or the Scripture which attests revelation" (Karl Barth, *Church Dogmatics*, 120–21).

211. von Allmen, *Preaching & Congregation*, 23–24.

212. von Allmen, *Pastorale du Baptême*, II.2.a

is the Amen of the congregation—their "yes" to the apostolic witness. In the saying of the creed, the church "gives back to God in its wholeness that Word which He addressed to it in the Gospel."[213] By such confession, the church not only gives assent to the apostolic witness; it pledges itself to "shoulder the consequences" of this confession, it promises to serve God in the world.[214] And this points us to the final aspect of apostolicity seen in von Allmen's writing: a missional apostolicity. It is here we incorporate some discussion of the church's activity in the world.

Missional

Though von Allmen affirms apostolicity as foundational, institutional, and doctrinal throughout his writings, when he most explicitly addresses the issue of ecclesial apostolicity, his emphasis is on the church's primary vocation to be a people sent to announce, point to, and manifest the reign of God—to join God's mission in the world. In a discussion in *Worship*, where von Allmen is cataloguing descriptive adjectives for the church (a list we will look at in the section below), he writes that it is finally an "apostolic or missionary"[215] community, effectively equating the two terms. Though it is "set apart" from the world, it is so in order that it may "enter the world to be salt and light therein."[216] Through its liturgical ministry, the church is open to heaven, but through its apostolic ministry, it is "open to the world."[217]

Interestingly, it is *in and through* its liturgical ministry in worship that the church emerges and becomes aware of itself as a missional/apostolic community. It does so according to von Allmen because in worship it finds itself separated from the rest of the world, from the "profanity of the milieu in which it is normally immersed," to use a phrase of Barth, quoted by von Allmen.[218] This differentiation happens first because the church embraces

213. It is worth noting that von Allmen is keen to reject the "cocktails of Biblical passages which have recently been introduced" as substitutes for the creed, both because of deficiency of content (they typically "invite the Church to stop up its ears when God has anything to say to it which is irritating to rationalism") or form ("a confession of faith is not a series of irresponsible, parrot-like repetitions"). See von Allmen, *Worship*, 166.

214. von Allmen, *Worship*, 166.

215. von Allmen, *Worship*, 51.

216. von Allmen, *Lord's Supper*, 39.

217. von Allmen, *Worship*, 154.

218. von Allmen, *Worship*, 51.

not all people in worship, but only the baptized. The church's existence, for those outside of it, is both threat and promise. And the Supper that is at the heart of worship is not, for von Allmen, a missionary exercise, but it establishes "the home base from which the church is sent to bear the sufferings and glory of Christ."[219]

The differentiation between church and world is evident in worship not only by the baptismal winnowing but also because the church gathers "on a particular day." According to the animal-lover von Allmen, the church is like a whale or dolphin that comes up for air and then dives back into the world from which it came and to which it is sent. The church at worship becomes aware of itself as the first fruits, not the totality. It recognizes itself as a gathered community distinct from the world. And it gathers on a particular day, not all days: "The cult is an epiphany of the church as a missionary community in the sense that it obliges the church to send forth into the world throughout the rest of the week those whom it has assembled out of the world on the first day."[220]

Von Allmen is comfortable making reference to the church's apostolicity in a number of different ways—foundational, institutional, and doctrinal. Yet his emphasis is on the church's *missional* apostolicity. He summarizes this way:

> Because Jesus Christ is the final and recapitulatory Word that God has spoken to the world, the Church, when it meets him in its worship, learns thereby that it is an apostolic or missionary community. It learns, therefore, that its Sunday gathering is not yet the Great Ingathering of the End, but rather the time and place from which the Church will return into the world, expressly commissioned to be dispersed in the world, to penetrate it in every part, to live there on the Christ who has given himself to the Church, in order to make him known and loved in the world; expressly commissioned also to say to men that the gospel is for them also, and that in this gospel they will find that which in the end will vindicate them and satisfy them.[221]

We now turn briefly to the liturgical markers of this apostolicity— where they may be found—before exploring in more detail the various activities to which the church is called *outside* of worship.

---

219. von Allmen, *Lord's Supper*, 111.

220. von Allmen, *Worship*, 51.

221. von Allmen, "Theological Frame," 13.

Liturgical Markers

Jean-Jacques von Allmen has less to say directly about the ways in which worship—in ritual, prayer, preaching, or sacrament—exhibits or reinforces ecclesial apostolicity than he had to say about the other Nicene marks. The markers of *institutional* apostolicity—ordination and the laying on of hands—are not treated in the volumes under our consideration, which deal with ordinary Christian worship rather than the occasional ecclesiastical ceremony.[222] The liturgical markers of *doctrinal* apostolicity are most evident in the congregational affirmation of the creed, which has already been discussed, and in preaching.

In some ways, *all* that he has to say about worship points to the church's *foundational* apostolicity. And perhaps every congregation would claim affirmative answers to questions of apostolicity: are the ministers part of one holy catholic church? Does the worship service proclaim the gospel message? Does the congregation leave worship to engage in God's work in the world? For von Allmen, one explicit marker of the apostolicity of the church's worship is that in both shape and content it is to be bound by the norm of Scripture and the testimony of the Apostles to Jesus. He writes that while the New Testament does not contain the liturgy of the apostolic church, it "marks the limits within which, with more or less felicity or obedience, Christian worship can truly be carried out as Christian worship." He enumerates them, following the pattern of Acts 2:42. First, the assembly must take place in the name of Jesus Christ, intending to be, in fact, Christian worship. Second, it must "enable the faithful to persevere in the teaching of the apostles." Third, it must enable them to commune, through the Lord's Supper, with the body of Christ. Fourth, it must pray together, offering up its petitions and thanksgivings to God. Fifth, it should be an assembly committed not just to these things, but also to a common life together.[223]

Unfortunately, we see very little in von Allmen articulating where in the activities of the church—either in its worship life or outside of it—that its *missional* apostolicity might be manifest. One can hardly blame him, as few of his contemporaries were doing so. But as we have seen, an exploration of what the church does in addition to what it is has been a feature of

---

222. As we have noted, however, von Allmen does speak of ordination more specifically in "Ordination: A Sacrament? a Protestant Reply," 40–48.

223. von Allmen, *Worship*, 96.

many ecclesiological projects throughout history, including many known to von Allmen. Hence, this is one of the areas where there is the most promise for work in the future. The pages that follow turn to explore briefly in this direction.

SUMMARY: MISSIONAL APOSTOLICITY AND ECCLESIAL ACTIVITY

The *Gospel In Our Culture Network* has suggested that the Nicene marks might be better understood in reverse order.[224] On this view, the church's apostolic mission is its primary identifying characteristic. It is the people sent to announce, point to, and manifest the reign of God. This implies not only *identity*, but *activity*; imperatives that flow from the indicatives. To follow the rest of the Nicene marks, then, the church is the people who proclaim, who reconcile, who sanctify, and who unify.

But what are the activities they do to fulfill this vocation? Some of them they do within the sanctuary, in her worship, her preaching, her celebration of the sacraments. Even missionary preaching is done, according to von Allmen, in the sanctuary. But there are a whole range of activities outside of Sunday worship in which the church engages that fulfill this call to missional apostolicity (as well as what one might call missional catholicity, holiness, and unity). Given von Allmen's starting point of *worship* as the epiphany of the church, it is not surprising to find a great deal in these works on the theological meaning of the ministry of worship (λατρεία), preaching (κήρυγμα), and sacraments (μυστήριον); and likewise less on extra-liturgical activities: upbuilding (οικοδομε), missionary proclamation (ευαγγέλιο), and service (διακονια), not to mention self-governance or polity (διατάσσω). To put it another way, one expects that in works on liturgy, preaching, and the sacraments, von Allmen would go into great detail exploring the theological meaning and purpose of the liturgical *confetior* or the secondary symbolic gestures used in a baptismal rite. Likewise, it is unsurprising, if disappointing, that he does *not* speak much of the church's extra-liturgical activities. There is very little in von Allmen acknowledging, for example, common ecclesial practices of *koinonia* and service; nothing about small spiritual accountability groups, the men's prayer breakfast, or the potluck supper; nothing about the youth service trip to Haiti, the food

---

224. See Guder, *Missional Church,* 248–68. My colleague George Hunsberger, one of the founders of the Gospel in Our Culture Network, is often credited for this innovation.

pantry, or the missionaries the church supports whose primary work is community development.

In von Allmen's liturgical ecclesiology, worship is the "time and place par excellence at which [the church] finds its own deep identity." But it is also, by his own admission, the place where it "learns how to be itself in its obedience *outside the sphere of worship as well*."[225] If this is the case, one might expect more, even in his writing on liturgy, on how these extra-liturgical obediences are reflected, distilled, expressed, and nurtured within worship. For it is in worship where our Monday-to-Saturday lives are shaped in Christ-like ways; where we practice postures of quiet, prayerful attentiveness; where we walk in paths of communal servanthood; where we acquire and hone dispositions of empathy and gratitude; where we exercise humility and acknowledge finitude; and where we map our joy to its source in God.

Jean-Jacques von Allmen certainly recognizes the importance of connecting worship to the church's life in the world. We recall his remarks about the church's identity as a diaconal community. There are a few gestures here and there in this direction. For example, in a section on the appropriate place for "notices" or announcements in worship, he indicates his preference for their placement after the sermon and before the prayers of intercession in order to offer concrete concerns for the prayer. By so doing, these announcements show "proof that if the Church disperses between the Sundays it does not therefore disappear, but that it continues to pray, to bear witness, to hear the Word of the Lord to live and to die under His watchful gaze."[226]

Despite such gestures, the relative neglect of the way in which the church's extra-liturgical life finds expression in worship, where its missional apostolicity becomes manifest in the Lord's Day assembly, opens von Allmen up to charges of an anachronistic Constantinian insularity. A more robust liturgical ecclesiology, emerging from von Allmen's key insights and building further upon it, would do well to start here. In other words, though it is outside the scope of this book, there would be value in further developing a liturgical ecclesiology that began with apostolicity—the way Barth or Guder might suggest—in order to explore what it means liturgically for the church to be a sent community that is catholic in scope and spirit, set apart to be holy, and unified in purpose and in its life.

---

225. von Allmen, "Theological Frame," 12. Emphasis added.

226. von Allmen, *Worship*, 176.

Moving toward pastoral liturgical ecclesiology. This work has examined the primary works on liturgy, preaching, and the sacraments written by Jean-Jacques von Allmen, along with a handful of important articles. In them, we have discerned and articulated his liturgical ecclesiology, built with a methodology that is fundamentally ecclesiological and pastoral. That work is marked by three central insights. First, that the church is made most manifest when God's people gather to worship. Second, that when the church gathers to worship, it recapitulates in its liturgy the story of God's salvation history. Finally, that the church's relationship to the world is therefore one of both threat and promise. The Nicene marks of the church were the next focus of our inquiry, to see how they might serve to illuminate and shape von Allmen's ecclesiologically-focused liturgical theology.

Jean-Jacques von Allmen's writings give evidence that he thought about various aspects of ecclesial unity: relational, pneumatological, eschatological, Christological, theological, sacramental, missional, and organizational. The second Nicene mark is also a multi-faceted theme, and our discussion identified four ways of thinking about ecclesial holiness: holiness as separation, holiness as perfection, holiness as dedication, and holiness as representation. The church's catholicity, according to von Allmen, has five aspects that we investigated: sociological, anthropological, spatial, temporal, and liturgical. Finally, in an exploration of the last mark (or the first mark?), we noted that von Allmen sounded notes of foundational, institutional, theological, and missional apostolicity.

Apparent along the way were various areas in the church's preaching, worship, and sacramental celebration where these marks are manifested. We noted where von Allmen's approach was strong and a few areas where a fully-orbed liturgical ecclesiology would require additional work.

We turn now from a constructive liturgical ecclesiology to what Gordon Lathrop called a "pastoral" liturgical ecclesiology—i.e., "secondary" theological work "turned especially toward the continuing reform of worship."[227]

227. Lathrop, *Holy People*, 7–8.

Chapter 5

Liturgical & Homiletical Implications

We enter the sanctuary like children filled with adoration, carrying our ineptly cooked but lovingly prepared liturgical breakfast. On the menu are prayers of which we know not the depth, sermons barely finished, hymns haltingly sung, the Word clumsily spoken. And there is God, like a parent patiently waiting to receive with relish and grace and kindness the burnt offerings we bring.

—TOM LONG, *WORSHIP WARS*, IX

PASTORAL LITURGICAL THEOLOGY. EARLIER I established that liturgical theology (including a liturgical ecclesiology) has to do not only with *naming* what happens in worship but also with *norming* that activity. It is both descriptive and prescriptive. The liturgical theologian serves the church by offering suggestions for ways in which its worship can honor God more fully, express the faith more richly, fulfill God's purposes for worship more adequately, and be made more transparent to God's presence in the assembly. The liturgical ecclesiologist offers suggestions for ways in which the church's worship can better express and shape the church's unity, holiness, catholicity, and apostolicity.

This study has identified various places where von Allmen's liturgical ecclesiology might find expression in the church's worship, preaching, and sacramental celebration. For example, we noted the importance of cross-cultural music in worship as a way of underscoring the church's temporal and spatial catholicity. What follows are some modest contributions in the direction of a pastoral liturgical ecclesiology.

First on the agenda are a few issues related to the Lord's Day and its typical *ordo*. Then, we will offer some reflections on discerning what makes for "good" worship, taking a cue both from von Allmen's ecclesiology and his methodology. The next section looks at baptism, the Lord's Supper, and preaching, in each case making some observations, and follows by putting forward a simple proposal, either descriptive or prescriptive. In each case, we will select a feature or two of von Allmen's liturgical ecclesiology, either directly related to the Nicene marks or related to his three primary theological themes, and give them application in a way that is either descriptive of a particular worshipping context and its practices, or provisionally prescriptive for wider consideration among churches in many contexts. The offerings here are not comprehensive. Yet they do suggest some possibilities and the promise of more fruitful work to be done in the future. Together, they help to demonstrate the enduring value of Jean-Jacques von Allmen as a conversation partner in the field of liturgical ecclesiology and his significance in the ongoing task of reforming the church's worship life.

ORDO & SALVATION HISTORY

James K. A. Smith, the philosopher turned liturgical theologian, writes in *Imagining the Kingdom* about the importance of liturgical form:

> Worship is not just the dissemination of some content or the expression of an 'inner' feeling, the very form of worship tells the Story. The form of worship is the logic of the practice; as such, it has a coherence that is fundamentally narrative, not deductive. The narrative arc of Christian worship is how it "makes sense," and it is through our immersion in the implicit narrative logic of the practice that the "practical sense" of the Christian Story soaks into our imagination and becomes part of our constituting background, the Story that governs our habitus.[1]

Though he does not credit von Allmen, Smith might well be channeling his Swiss Reformed predecessor in his insistence upon the fundamentally narrative character of worship. Von Allmen articulated his conviction in terms of salvation history and worship as a recapitulation of that history. This next section will look briefly at three issues and make

1. Smith, *Imagining the Kingdom*, 169.

three recommendations related to ordinary Lord's Day worship: word and table, sequence and juxtaposition, and gathering and sending rites. We will demonstrate along the way, how these issues and recommendations flow from or resonate with elements of von Allmen's liturgical ecclesiology, including both the Nicene marks and von Allmen's central theological themes.

Word & Table

Von Allmen, both as a parish pastor and as a university theologian, insisted that the regular order of worship on the Lord's Day include both apostolic witness—i.e., the proclamation of the Word—and weekly Communion in the body and blood of Christ. This has not been the pattern in most branches of the Reformed family, in which the Lord's Supper is celebrated quarterly or perhaps monthly, and the resulting truncated service is really a "Sunday preaching service in which the elements are more or less strung together without any structural relatedness."[2]

But von Allmen was part of a chorus of churchmen, from both Reformed and other Protestant families, insisting on the importance of reclaiming the ancient pattern. His conviction is grounded partly in an acknowledgement of its historical significance and widespread synchronic and diachronic practice—what we have seen, in our discussion of the Nicene marks, as sacramental unity. It also is grounded in "distinctive holiness," as the table marks the "difference between the world in a way which is not subjective, self-centered, and moralizing, but objective."[3] But more importantly, von Allmen's dogged insistence on restoring this liturgical *ordo* to the church flows from his sense of foundational apostolicity—i.e., that the church's liturgical life best follows the pattern set in the apostolic witness of scripture and in Jesus' own earthly life. The gospels divide Jesus' life into Galilean and Jerusalemite phases, corresponding to the "Mass of the catechumens" and the "Mass of the faithful."

At nearly every opportunity in his books on worship and the Lord's Supper—and even on preaching—von Allmen argues the imperative need for the church to reclaim this essential liturgical structure.[4] He speaks in

2. Hageman, *Pulpit and Table*, 33.

3. von Allmen, *Worship*, 155.

4. See, for example, the chapter on "Sermon in Worship," where von Allmen says: "The worship of the Church is not complete unless the sacrament accompanies the

particular to Reformed churches, bemoaning the "atrophy of our sacramental life."[5] The Reformed churches, "alone among the great liturgical traditions, [have] excluded from [their] regular Sunday worship the celebration of the Lord's Supper."[6] Von Allmen argues vigorously for the absolute necessity of the Eucharist for Reformed worship.[7] It is necessary because Christ instituted and commanded it, because it gives authentic substance to the prophetic and teaching ministry of the Word, and because it enables us to mark the difference between the church and the world. Von Allmen goes so far as to say that "not only is the Eucharist necessary to the cult, but that the abandonment of it is an abandonment of the very substance of the cult."[8] The word and sacrament are a unity. They reinforce and point to one another. The table is not merely a response to the word, they are a unity of Christ's presence.[9] While the church has great freedom in how it chooses to order its worship, says von Allmen, "we have no right— that is, if we wish to remain a Church that is Reformed according to the Word of God—to confirm our confessional liturgical peculiarities in their

---

sermon; for the sermon has as much need of the sacrament as the sacrament has of the sermon" (von Allmen, *Preaching*, 40).

5. The place of the table in the worship of Reformed churches has been problematic for centuries, a story detailed in Howard Hagemann's *Pulpit & Table*. That book rehearses the battle between the competing sacramental theologies of Calvin and Zwingli, and how the logical liturgical consequence of Calvin's doctrine of the Real Presence of Christ at the table—weekly Eucharist—was outflanked in the practice of Reformed churches by Zwingli's dualistic memorialism and its consequent quarterly celebration.

6. von Allmen, *Worship*, 152. Zwingli believed that only the spiritual could convey the reality of God, who is Spirit. Thus, only preaching can function to communicate Christ's presence; the meal is material and not a fit vehicle for the spiritual; it merely functions in a thin, memorial way. This was the theological viewpoint that became enshrined in Reformed church practice even though Calvin's doctrine of the Supper—that the Holy Spirit in the meal lifts us into the Real Presence of Christ—is the one most Reformed churches hold to in theory.

7. I would say that this is the *primary* argument of the entire work. Here are the book's concluding words: "Let all those who do not wish our Church, reformed according to God's word, to die . . . let them apply to the authorities of the church, demanding the re-introduction of the weekly communion service. . . . If we are unwilling to obey Jesus Christ through the restoration of the weekly Eucharist, then the day will soon come when even what we have will be taken from us" (von Allmen, *Worship*, 313–14).

8. von Allmen, *Worship*, 155.

9. von Allmen, *Worship*, 154–55.

most notorious features, that is, in their breaking of the normal rhythm of Christian worship."[10]

It was one of the great joys of his life that his own Swiss Reformed church finally declared that the celebration of the Eucharist be part of the normative pattern of Lord's Day worship. Among one branch of the Reformed church family to which I belong—the Dutch Reformed Church in America, now the Reformed Church in America (RCA)—the prescribed order for worship has most often been articulated as a three-fold pattern: 1) the Approach to the Word, 2) the Proclamation of the Word, and 3) the Response to the Word.[11] While one might include the table in the third section, von Allmen explicitly avoids using a three-fold pattern precisely because it so clearly privileges the Word to the possible exclusion of the table.

Thus, an obvious starting point for a pastoral liturgical ecclesiology based in the work of von Allmen is to join him in commending the weekly celebration of the Lord's Supper as a necessary part of the worship which forms an assembly of people to be the church, in unity with the foundational apostolic pattern.[12]

Sequence & Juxtaposition

Beyond the inclusion of both word and table in weekly worship, are there other recommendations of von Allmen's liturgical ecclesiology that one might make to congregations seeking to put into practice the insights for a church at worship? How do we today step into God's past, present, and future? Von Allmen does not say much about the order in which elements of worship should be celebrated. There should be some structure, to be sure, and he admits that some structures are better than others (more

10. von Allmen, *Worship*, 287.

11. Others in the Reformed family (the PCUSA, for instance) articulate this same pulse-beat in four movements, changing the third movement from the more generic "response" to the specific "table" and appending a "sending" afterwards.

12. The Commission on Worship in the Reformed Church in America is presently undertaking a revision of its own Liturgy and Directory for Worship. These documents are deemed "constitutional," i.e., directive and binding for clergy. The will of the commission at present is to push for the same sort of change von Allmen did more than fifty years ago in Switzerland.

"intelligent" or more "fervent"), but he avoids pronouncing blessing on a particular configuration of worship actions.[13]

Yet it might make sense that there be some resonance in worship with a sense of God's work in history. Thus, one could imagine—and commend—worship services that begin where scripture begins, where the story begins: with some praise rooted in God's character and person as Creator. Following the contours of salvation history, a penitential parabola might follow, taking the congregation into the depths of humble confession and up out of them into the light of God's grace. Following this moment might be a kerygmatic, Christocentric sermon followed by a sacramental celebration of Jesus' life, death, and resurrection. The service might well conclude eschatologically, reminding the congregation of their Kingdom trajectory.

Gathering & Sending

Jean-Jacques von Allmen's liturgical ecclesiology might commend a more explicit way of helping to nurture the sense that when a congregation comes to worship, they are stepping into God's grand history of salvation. One way to signal this important truth is to begin and conclude services with fittingly narrative words and gestures. At the start of worship, says von Allmen, two options are common in the liturgical tradition. One is a greeting, spoken by the presider on behalf of God.[14] It often takes the form of words—apostolic words—lifted from one of the scriptural epistles: "Grace and peace be unto you from God our Father and the Lord Jesus Christ." The other option is an invocation, an epicletic prayer expressing the church's *Maranatha*. These sound notes of foundational apostolicity (grounding the very beginning of the service in scripture) and, depending on the words that are used, may also sound notes of holiness that indicate the people gathered are set apart during this time.

But neither of these options is quite direct enough. Turning from prescriptive urging to descriptive commendation, what follows is one way that a community of believers might choose to begin a worship service in such a way as to highlight its narrative character, telling the story of salvation history at the very outset of worship. It is, in fact, one of our regular practices among the community of believers where I teach at Western Theological

13. von Allmen, *Worship*, 80, 181, 288.

14. This is one aspect of what von Allmen calls the "clerical" proclamation of the Word. See von Allmen, *Worship*, 137–41.

Seminary. I offer it here not as a paradigm to be deployed in any and every church context, but simply as one example of this recommendation finding expression in a particular community.

Our services typically begin by attending to four central objects with symbolic meaning: a single candle, a Bible, a cross, and finally a font. God's story of salvation is told as we light the candle, bring the Bible from a congregant to the pulpit, drape the cross with a swag of cloth in the appropriate liturgical season, and finally pour water into the baptismal font. The story is told in words something like this:[15]

> ONE: The Lord be with you.
> *ALL: And also with you.*
> Lord, open our lips.
> *And our mouths will proclaim your praise.*
> Your love and mercy never cease.
> *Fresh as the morning and sure as the sunrise.*
>
> God of grace and glory,
> In the beginning,
> You brought light from darkness [light candle],
> Created the world,
> Made us in your image,
> And set us on the Way.
> And so we praise you.
> *SUNG: Hallelujah, Lord Most High!*
>
> This would have been enough.
> But when we had lost the plot,
> You gave your Word to your chosen people [Bible from people to pulpit],
> To show us the Way.
> And so we praise you.
> *SUNG: Hallelujah, Lord Most High!*
>
> This would have been enough.
> But you came among us,
> And stretched out your arms [swag fabric on cross]
> To fulfill that Way.
> And so we praise you.
> *SUNG: Hallelujah, Lord Most High!*
>
> This would have been enough.
> But you sent your Spirit
> to cleanse us, renew us,

15. Many will recognize the refrain in this responsive reading to be an adaptation of the Jewish Passover song, "Dayenu."

And to join us to that Way [pour water into the font].
And so we praise you.
SUNG: *Hallelujah, Lord Most High!*

We return to these same symbols at the close of each service and say words that point to the church's missional apostolicity, i.e, our vocation as sent people. The words vary from season to season—but the gestures convey the meaning: the candle is blown out into a cupped hand, which is then opened in a sweeping gesture toward the congregation, indicating that Christ's light now shines in them as they go into the world. The Bible is brought back and given to one of the congregants. The swag of fabric is taken from the cross and placed like a stole around the neck of another congregant, to signify the servant-life we are now called to live in the world. Finally, water from the font is sprinkled on to the congregation, encouraging them to "live wet," a baptized and baptismal people. This is the sort of liturgical expression of the church's extra-worship activity that fills in the lacuna we noted in von Allmen's liturgical ecclesiology.

SACRAMENTAL PREACHING

The significance of both preaching and worship in von Allmen's liturgical ecclesiology has been a regular theme in this book. We have also seen how von Allmen emphasized the unity of Word and Sacrament in the liturgical *ordo*—how the church is ill-formed when it minimizes or eliminates from its weekly worship either proclamation or the Eucharist.[16] But von Allmen's convictions about the unity of Word and Sacrament go deeper. Preaching is, for von Allmen, a sacramental liturgical action. What does this mean?

The Reformed tradition, in which von Allmen locates himself, has always claimed a very high view of preaching as a means of grace, of God's self-disclosure. *Predicatio Verbi est Verbum Dei*, according to the Second Helvetic Confession. Or, as von Allmen puts it, "Christian preaching is not simply a meditation on the Word of God. It is a proclamation of that Word,

---

16. "This twofold necessity of preaching and the Eucharist is perhaps the most powerful demonstration of the dialectical situation of the Church; it is no longer of the world (hence it already has access to the heavenly banquet), but it is still in the world (hence it needs the warnings, the encouragements, the teachings, and the consolations of preaching)" (von Allmen, *Worship*, 146).

it implies a divine miracle."[17] The nature of that miracle, he argues, is the same as that of the sacraments—it makes God's living Word present:

> This interpretation of God's work in our preaching establishes its connexion with the sacraments, and consequently—contemporary homiletics insists ever more strongly on this—recognizes in preaching a sacramental aspect. This is one of the many reasons why we should not suggest any opposition between preaching and the sacraments, why we should rather, in view of the miracle of the incarnation, give the doctrine of the Word of God an interpretation which is at once homiletic and baptismal or Eucharistic.[18]

The next section offers some von Allmen-based reflections on what sacramental preaching is—i.e., a theology of sacramental preaching—and then some practical suggestions for how it might be pursued by those whose weekly task is to witness to the living Word among the community animated by him and the Spirit which makes him known. We will consider four ways that preaching and the sacraments relate to one another: preaching *as* a sacrament; preaching *to* the sacraments; preaching with a sacramental eye; and preaching about the sacraments.

Preaching as Sacrament

Sacraments, according to the Reformed tradition, "are visible, holy signs and seals. They were instituted by God so that by our use of them he might make us understand more clearly the promise of the gospel, and seal that promise."[19] We might expand this tight definition by identifying four sacramental features. Sacraments are 1) instituted by God; 2) simultaneously earthly and divine; 3) point to Christ; and 4) accompanied by a promise.[20] We will look briefly at each of these points to see how preaching meets these criteria in von Allmen's homiletical theology.

Preaching is instituted by God. Again and again in scripture, the one sent to speak a prophetic word has received a divine call. "The word of the Lord came to me" and "Say thus to my people" are formulaic phrases throughout the Old Testament, conveying God's initiative in the prophetic proclamation. Likewise in the New Testament, Jesus commands the

17. von Allmen, *Worship*, 144–45.
18. von Allmen, *Preaching & Congregation*, 8.
19. "Heidelberg Catechism," s.v. "Q&A 66."
20. Vander Zee, *Christ, Baptism, and the Lord's Supper*, 27–36

disciples to "Go . . . and teach" (as well as baptize). Paul insists in 2 Corinthians that he is not preaching himself, but God (2 Cor 4:5). He likewise maintains that he did not choose the task for himself, but was called to it. The boldness of preachers is founded upon their conviction that, as von Allmen wrote: "The authorization to preach comes from an order of the Lord Himself."[21]

Preaching is simultaneously earthly and divine. In baptism, ordinary water—from a river, lake, or faucet—becomes the bath of forgiveness, the "laver of salvation," and the womb of new life. In the Lord's Supper, ordinary bread and wine become for communicants participation in the body and blood of Jesus.[22] Just so, in preaching, ordinary human words become the "vehicle which God has chosen to make his own Word resound."[23] The activity of preaching is both humble and glorified, everyday and eternal.

Von Allmen illustrates the point using the Chalcedonian Christological formula: true God and true human, unconfusedly, unchangeably, indivisibly, and inseparately. Just so, in preaching, "the Word of God resounds in, under, and with the words of the messenger, without those words ceasing in consequence to be completely human."[24] In a similar (and somewhat ironic way),[25] von Allmen compares the preacher to the Virgin Mary:

> The mystery of preaching reflects the mystery of the conception and birth of Jesus, and there is no deeper pattern for the spirituality of the preacher than that of the Virgin Mary, who receives, clothes with her substance and gives forth to the world, God's eternal Word, true God and true man.[26]

Preaching points to Christ. Karl Barth related the proclaimed word of God to the scriptural Word of God and to the revealed eternal logos of God as three concentric circles, with each expanding ring pointing to the center. Von Allmen's theology of preaching resonates with that of his friend Barth:

---

21. von Allmen, *Preaching & Congregation*, 14.

22. I am careful in my language here to use a Eucharistic formulation that is in line with von Allmen's reformed convictions.

23. von Allmen, *Preaching & Congregation*, 12.

24. von Allmen, *Preaching & Congregation*, 12.

25. The comparison is ironic because von Allmen did not believe that it is theologically appropriate for a woman to hold the ecclesial office. See von Allmen, "Est-il legitimate de consacrer," 5–28, and von Allmen, "Women and the Threefold Ministry," 88–99.

26. von Allmen, *Worship*, 143–44.

> We must therefore not expect any other Word from God than
> that which He has sufficiently pronounced in the story of the
> birth, ministry, passion, victory, and glory of Jesus the Jew, from
> Nazareth in Palestine, who lived nearly two thousand years ago.[27]

Von Allmen insists that preaching must be based in scripture and point, as scripture does, to Christ.

Furthermore, von Allmen contends, preaching today is the *continuation* of Jesus' preaching, and it looks forward to the word Jesus will speak at his return. Just as in worship, God is not merely the object, but the subject. In a world where preaching can often be compared to teaching, therapy, or politics, sacramental preaching insists that it find its appropriate center at the one in whom all things hold together.

Finally, preaching declares a promise. "An authentic sermon," von Allmen says, "is an eschatological event." The promise of the Gospel, the kerygma of salvation offered in Christ (and thus in preaching), comes always with both the offer of mercy and its paradoxical twin, a threat and a call to renunciation. Thus, von Allmen says that when someone hears the Word, their "salvation is at stake."[28] The pinch of these two is what commands a decision on the part of the hearers of the word, and provides the window through which the Spirit can do her sanctifying work. Thus, the promise declared in preaching is not just eternal life (though it is that) but also transformation today: stronger faith, deeper discipleship, and action rooted in love—in sum, transformation into greater Christlikeness.

Preaching to the Sacraments

In addition to the sacramental *character* of preaching, the second key theological feature of von Allmen's notion of "sacramental preaching" is its sacramental aim, derived in part from ecclesial unity and in part from missional unity: "The preaching of the Word has in fact always a sacramental purpose, it ever seeks as its end a sacrament which will confirm and seal it, or rather, prove that it has borne fruit." This recalls our discussion of von Allmen's distinction between "missionary" and "liturgical" preaching, preaching that is intended either to regenerate or to edify and build up the body of Christ:

27. von Allmen, *Preaching & Congregation*, 22.
28. von Allmen, *Preaching & Congregation*, 17.

If it is non-liturgic missionary preaching, it aims at the sacrament of baptism; if it is parochial, liturgical preaching, it is orientated towards the Eucharist. That is why, if the proclamation of the Word of God is necessary to the Eucharist to prevent it from becoming self-centered and magical, the Eucharist is necessary to preaching to prevent it from degenerating into self-centered intellectualism or mere chat.[29]

The theology of sacramental preaching just articulated from von Allmen reflects very well, unsurprisingly, the liturgical ecclesiology discerned in his work. For example, our discussion reflecting his insistence on the sacramental aims of preaching resonates with notes of the spatial and temporal catholicity as the church is called by the word to be a Eucharistic and baptismal community. Likewise, the threat-character of preaching calls the church to a sanctifying holiness. In the centrality of the gospel message, we hear notes of foundational apostolicity and eschatological unity.

But sacramental preaching is more than a theology of preaching; it is also a practice. And in this respect, von Allmen offers less help than one might like. In a recent work, Todd Townshend says:

Even von Allmen . . . who insists on the sacramental character of preaching, does not give any direction to preachers indicating how these shifts in understanding may be put into the practice of liturgical/sacramental preaching. He simply points to the possibility of 'sacramental ways of thinking about homiletics.'[30]

Here, then, are three ways to put into practice the type of sacramental preaching von Allmen wrote about as central to the church's identity and mission. The first flows naturally, and somewhat obviously, from the second theological insight, that preaching has a sacramental *telos*. If preaching indeed "aims" at either baptism or the Lord's Supper in a theological way, then a sermon should actually conclude with a "move"—in both a rhetorical and physical way—toward the sacrament in view. If a sermon sounds ecclesial notes of Christological unity, dedicatory holiness, sociological catholicity, or missional apostolicity—or if it concludes fittingly with a call to discipleship,[31] renunciation or admission of guilt, or commitment and

29. von Allmen, *Worship*, 144.

30. Townshend, *Sacramentality of Preaching*, 22.

31. Curiously, the common term for a call to new or renewed discipleship is an "altar" call, when the more appropriate piece of liturgical furniture to have in mind is the font.

accountability—a preacher could step to the font during the last paragraph, dip her hands in the water, and either remind the congregation of their own baptisms or call those unbaptized to the new life offered in Christ. For example, a sermon on Joshua 24 ("as for me and my house") or from Philippians 2 ("work out your own salvation") might well conclude at the font. Likewise, a sermon whose theme resonates with Eucharistic themes—remembrance, communion, and hope—eschatological unity, anthropological catholicity, or theological apostolicity might fittingly end with a short stroll from the pulpit to the table. A sermon on Psalm 133 ("How good and pleasant"), for example, or Matthew 17 (the Transfiguration) can very beautifully be turned toward the glory of the presence of Christ at communion.

Preaching with a Sacramental Eye

A second practical means of preaching sacramentally is for the preacher to be on the constant look-out for sacramental resonances in the texts that are preached. Scriptural passages that have food or water in them are surprisingly common, whether or not they have explicit sacramental overtones. The pastor who is preaching sacramentally sees the Eucharist in every meal, baptism in every body of water. The food may be the post-resurrection fish fry in John 21, or the pancake breakfast in 1 Kings 17; the water may be the still waters of Psalm 23 or troubled waters of Isaiah 43. A new depth of meaning may be discovered by viewing these texts through a sacramental lens.

But more than this, the scriptures testify to the inherent goodness of the physical world, and the significance of material signs help us to be reminded of Gospel truths or to encounter God. This is especially important for congregations that tend to make the exercise of religion—and worship in particular—a merely cognitive or Gnostic exercise. The preacher who speaks of rocks and fire and grass and skin is preaching sacramentally. He reminds us that we are material and that creation is good, that matter matters to God. The preacher who does this helps his congregation to cultivate a sacramental way of life, one that assumes God is present to be encountered in every moment, that is open and willing to be surprised, confused, or amazed by the extraordinary in the ordinary.[32]

32. One might also consider preaching with an eye for seeing God acting in the world in the same way that God acts in the text proclaimed. See Wilson, *Four Pages of the*

Preaching About the Sacraments

Finally, the pastor who wishes to preach sacramentally will not neglect to preach occasionally *about* the sacraments, to help explore the full range of theological meanings the sacraments carry, and to connect them with the lives of those in their charge. Individuals and congregations often have truncated understandings of the sacraments—e.g., baptism is about washing away sins, communion is about Jesus' death. These are not incorrect, just incomplete. Baptism is also about the gifting of the Holy Spirit, about union with Christ in death and new life, about adoption into the church. Likewise, the Lord's Supper has multiple meanings. In the formularies of my own Reformed Church in America, we speak of "remembrance, communion, and hope."[33] One might add to these three other themes: Thanksgiving, sacrifice, and presence. Sacramental preaching will identify and explore an abundance of sacramental meanings.

As Lester Ruth and Craig Satterlee point out, mystagogical preaching is different from other kinds of preaching in this way: first of all, it is "an exegesis of our sacramental and worship experience rather than Scripture itself." Certainly scripture remains central, but the sacramental preacher "names the dimensions of sacramental experience using biblical associations, cultural resonances, and natural images in creative ways."[34] This follows, in some ways, from the patristic period, in which the ecclesial mystogogy typically happened *after* catechumens were baptized and came to the table. Understanding the meaning of the sacraments, on this model, is not a prerequisite for participation; experience comes first, after which theological exploration deepens its meaning.

Conclusion

Congregations are blessed by having a preacher who takes the sacraments seriously. Such a preacher speaks with both the confidence and humility of knowing that the sermon is a sacramental encounter with the living Word

---

Sermon, or Hilkert, *Naming Grace.*

33. See Reformed Church in America, "Directory for Worship." Jean-Jacques von Allmen says, "We might specify in it the phases of the memorial of Christ's passion, of the irruption of the ESCHATON, and of communion" (von Allmen, *Worship*, 147). The WCC document, *Baptism, Eucharist, and Ministry,* offers a helpful summary of the many sacramental meanings its member churches embrace.

34. Satterlee and Ruth, *Creative Preaching On the Sacraments*, 134.

who, by the power of the Holy Spirit, animates it. Such a preacher understands that God's Word does not return empty, but that it has a purpose: to edify, to convert. Such a preacher reads scripture with a sacramental lens, seeing hints of the church's central mysteries in its stories, images, and objects. Such a preacher will explain and explore with the congregation a wide range of sacramental meanings and connect them with their own experiences of baptism and the Lord's Supper. Such a preacher will do all this, understanding that it is the same Word of God proclaimed, promised, and made present in both sign and sermon.

OPEN TABLE AND BAPTISMAL REMEMBRANCE

In 1998 and again in 2004, the General Assembly (the highest judicatory) of the PC (USA) received overtures from presbyteries to amend its Book of Order in the direction of an "open" table—i.e., to eliminate the requirement that those invited to the Lord's Supper be baptized Christians. The General Assembly acted by referring the overture to its Office of Theology and Worship, inviting them to report back after having thoroughly studied the issue.

The Office of Theology and Worship convened a study group that reported back to the General Assembly in 2006 with the publication "Invitation to Christ." This final report was not a recommendation for the liturgy or the Book of Order with regard to the Lord's Supper. Instead, it was a study guide and a series of recommendations for the church to "deepen baptismal identity and to reflect together on sacramental practice as they shed light on the church's identity and mission and give visible shape to our common life in Christ."[35]

In what follows, I will examine what "Invitation to Christ" has to say about the meaning of baptism, especially concerning open table practices, and put it in conversation with von Allmen's liturgical ecclesiology—more specifically, his sense of worship as both promise and threat and the way in which this informs a kind of distinctive ecclesial holiness. Both von Allmen and "Invitation" suggest that while infant baptism is certainly valid, the norm for Christians—especially in a post-Christendom context—might well be to move in the direction of offering baptism primarily to believing, professing adults. I will then make a hard turn into pastoral liturgical ecclesiology, offering a specific liturgical practice to enhance the church's self-understanding of itself as a baptismal community.

35. Presbyterian Church, "Invitation to Christ," 9.

Open-Table

"Invitation to Christ" has a helpful section rehearsing biblical principles, themes, and examples related to baptism and the Lord's Supper. It summarizes the positions of those who both support and oppose opening the table to the unbaptized. Those who advocate for open table practice emphasize sociological catholicity of the church, what the report calls the inclusivity of God's welcome to all. Those who advocate against open table practice emphasize relational unity, or, in the report's words, "God's call of and ongoing relationship with a covenant community." "Invitation" recognizes the validity of both points of view based on faithful readings of scripture and the church's theological heritage. Its conclusion, however, is that "the fullest range of meanings of baptism and the Lord's Supper—both God's expansive love and forgiveness and the call to be a community of disciples, the body of Christ in the world—is preserved and embodied through the normative practice of baptism before Eucharist."[36] At the same time, it acknowledges a biblical 'cross-current' that would allow for the disruption of those practices when they serve exclusionary purposes.[37]

Distinctive Holiness: The People of God at Worship as both Threat and Promise. One of the central themes of von Allmen's theology is that the people of God at worship are, to the world, both a threat and a promise. It is a threat because it is a challenge to human righteousness, a foretaste of the last judgment, and a protest against idolatry. But it is also a promise because if the world can renounce itself, it can regain its true destiny. A key feature emerging from this theme in von Allmen's liturgical ecclesiology—a feature highlighted in his discussion of the church as a *baptismal* community—is the sense of distinguishing holiness: that the church is set apart from the world. The impulse to erase the distinction, says von Allmen, is born of a collapse or mistrust of eschatology.

Interestingly, this ecclesial theme is nowhere present in "Invitation to Christ." The promise is there, but the threat is downplayed. Yet von Allmen, were he a participant in this conversation, would insist that only

---

36. The section on history concludes similarly, noting that many of the PCUSA's ecumenical partners are also "exploring the practice of communing the unbaptized. Presently, they maintain that baptism normally precedes Eucharist. Many church bodies are encouraging congregational renewal through a recovery of deeper sacramental practices, especially a revitalized practice of baptism and baptismal renewal" (Presbyterian Church, "Invitation to Christ," 35).

37. Presbyterian Church, "Invitation to Christ," 23–24.

the baptized be invited to come to the table. "The Sacrament . . . simplifies and purifies the church's missionary obligation by delineating the frontier between the Church and the world."[38] The evangelistic impulse that would invite any believer, baptized or not, to the table, is born of a misunderstanding of the Eucharist—and of worship more generally. One of the functions of the Lord's Supper, says von Allmen, is not to mark how far the Word of God has gone, but how far it has been *received.*

> It is in this sense that the Supper is missionary: from the Supper, the Church is sent into the world to bear the sufferings and the glory of Christ because she is His Body and His Bride. Thus it is not the celebration itself which is missionary. This is reserved—at least in the very wise view of the ancient Church—for the baptized alone, for what takes place there would seem foolish and scandalous in the eyes of the world. It takes place behind closed doors, as at the time of its institution before, or at the time of its ratification after, the passion and glorification of Jesus. The desire to make of the Supper a missionary action seems to me to change the content of the Supper and to transform it into a *verbum visibile,* into a spectacle which no longer involves in communion those who are present. But if the Holy Table is the place from which the Church is sent out into the world, it is also the place to which she returns from the world, laden with her harvest like the disciples after the miraculous draught of fish, or like Israel coming back to the Promised Land after the hard struggles of the Exodus or returning after the Exile.[39]

Post-Christendom Recommendations. Both von Allmen and "Invitation to Christ" recognize that the post-Christian cultural situation in which the church now finds itself requires a re-consideration of its discipline (among other things).[40] More and more people, says "Invitation to Christ," are coming to worship, but they are not baptized. They are hungry for something, yet they are conditioned by an individualism, consumerism, and pluralism that do not well understand or submit to ecclesial discipline.[41] Von Allmen

38. von Allmen, *Lord's Supper,* 39.

39. von Allmen, *Lord's Supper,* 111.

40. "First, the Church is so used to a baptismal discipline ordered by the sociological conditions of an unquestioned Christianity that it has great difficulty adapting its discipline, and thus its practice, to the "post-Christian" situation where faith is no longer a given, baptism should not be a given either" (von Allmen, *Pastorale du Baptême,* Introduction).

41. Presbyterian Church, "Invitation to Christ," 51–55.

writes that the hope for Eucharistic discipline—e.g., an appropriate fencing of the table—is "idle" in the church that has abandoned baptismal discipline. He suggests that one of the most urgent tasks facing the churches today is to "join forces in order to subject baptismal practice to a criticism as radical and severe as was the criticism to which the Reformation subjected the Eucharistic practice of the Medieval West."[42]

Like his friend Barth, von Allmen stands, cross-armed and scowling at the widespread European practice of baptizing most infants. It is, he wrote, a "sociologically anachronistic and theologically irresponsible" practice.[43] He affirms infant baptism,[44] but says it has "limited legitimacy," under certain circumstances (including an insistence that children who have been baptized be admitted to the table).[45] His strong preference is for the church normally to baptize only those who have the ability to make their own profession of faith.[46]

At the same time, the need today is for deepened baptismal understanding in the church and deepened practice. "Invitation to Christ" concludes with the story of a pastor who said this: "I have long held the conviction that if I can just help people understand the significance of their baptisms, I will have done enough as pastor." In the same spirit, von Allmen writes that the liturgical renewal the church so desperately needs:

> will have as a necessary corollary a fresh awareness of baptism, a new understanding of the discipline necessary to be a community of baptized people, and a rediscovery of the grace given to such a community of knowing, amid the passing of the days of this world,

---

42. von Allmen, *Lord's Supper*, 38.

43. von Allmen, "Réflexions d'un Protestant," 66–86. See also von Allmen, "L'Eglise primitive et le baptême des enfants," 43–47; as well as "Inconveniences of Generalized Infant Baptism," in von Allmen, *Pastorale du Baptême*, III.4.

44. See especially von Allmen, *Pastorale du Baptême*, III.2.

45. von Allmen, *Worship*, 186–87.

46. "Finally, I believe that it is not necessary to hang on to the practice of widespread infant baptism because of the baptized individuals themselves. If in the past one could, without excessive scruples, integrate them in the *corpus christianum* without asking them their opinion, if it was possible to throw them into the world as Christians because this world was equipped culturally, politically, legally, even policed, in a way to protect their Christianity, it is no longer or it is less and less so the case today. Is it not the best time then to stop the practice of infant baptism? One must say yes" (von Allmen, *Pastorale du Baptême*, III.4.b).

the weekly recurrence of the Lord's Day, a day less for rest than for celebration.[47]

One Suggestion: Weekly Remembrance

The Presbyterian report "Invitation to Christ" recommended five practices to help nurture this deepened understanding and practice of the sacraments:

1. Set the font in full view of the congregation.

2. Open the font and fill it with water on every Lord's Day.

3. Set cup and plate on the Lord's Table on every Lord's Day.

4. Lead appropriate parts of weekly worship from the font and from the table.

5. Increase the number of Sundays on which the Lord's Supper is celebrated.[48]

Von Allmen, in thinking specifically about baptismal practice, recommended that on days when baptisms are to take place, two unusual groups of participants be invited to take part: first, those who were "baptized unawares when they were very young," and so that they "do not get re-baptized in a sect, the Church is obliged to offer a celebration which confirms their baptism, thereby giving it its existential meaning that was missing on the day when they were marked with the seal of Christ."[49] The second group is baptized adults, "for whom it is important to be reminded through a ritual that their baptism commits them for their entire life."[50]

---

47. von Allmen, "Theological Frame," 12–13.

48. Presbyterian Church, "Invitation to Christ," 5.

49. Jean-Jacques von Allmen answers the question of whether this is a rebaptism with this: "But if the aspect to be renewed is the commitment of the baptized individual: his renunciation of the Devil and his adherence to Christ? I think a renewal is possible here, since it is the only aspect of baptism which can also be denied. The role of the Lord in the covenant of baptism—the *sigillum ex parte Die* to cite J.-F. Ostervald—is irrevocable; the promises that God made then are firm and can be absolutely counted on; but the commitments that are made then by the baptized individual—the *sigillum ex parte nostril*—always remain threatened, are always in danger of being broken. This is why I think they are renewable, and that it is even a measure of good pastoral ministry to give believers the opportunity to renew them" (von Allmen, *Pastorale du Baptême*, IV.8.c).

50. von Allmen, *Pastorale du Baptême*, IV.8.b.

What follows, then, is a suggestion for one modest way this type of ritual renewal can be enfolded into the regular weekly Lord's Day liturgy of the church. Imagine a church, where just before the prayers of the people, the pastor (or other congregational representative) steps to the font and asks whose baptismal anniversaries fall in the coming week. A few hands go up. The pastor warmly invites these people to step forward to the front of the sanctuary. As they do so, they put their hands in the water at the font, remembering their own baptisms. The pastor touches them on the shoulder and begins the regular congregational prayers of thanksgiving and intercession by speaking their names and offering thanks to God for their particular gifts and for God's outpouring of grace in their lives. Maybe the pastor mentions one person's gift of compassion, another's gift for teaching, and another's gifts for organization and administration, exercised in her job at a non-profit organization. The prayer names their natural or spiritual gifts, mapping their source to the Holy Spirit, part of the baptismal gifting.

Now imagine Mary, Jim, or Claudia[51] approaching the pastor with their experiences of conversion and their requests to publicly and eagerly affirm their recommitment to Christ. Other special requests might be added to these—for instance, a nine-year-old eager to come for the first time to the Lord's Supper, a fifteen-year old making profession of faith, or a thirty-three-year-old going back to graduate school. The pastor who regularly remembers baptism at the prayers of the people now has a way to

---

51. The following names are not real, though their stories are:

Mary is eighteen years old. After her first year in college, she spent the summer doing mission work in the Yucatan peninsula. It was a transformative experience, as she was touched by the power and presence of the Holy Spirit, both in her life and among the people with whom she served. She thought she was a Christian before, but now—well, now things are completely different. So she approaches the pastor of her hometown Reformed church with a request: she wants to be re-baptized to mark her spiritual awakening.

Jim is forty-five. After hitting "rock bottom," he has admitted his dependency and has awakened from a fifteen-year drunken stupor. Though he has been part of the church all his life, he now sees with greater clarity than ever what it means to live in a community of Christ-followers in honesty, humility, and accountability—to try every day to live a life worthy of God's forgiving and transforming grace poured out "while we were yet sinners." He, too, approaches his pastor (within the Reformed tradition) with a request to mark his sobriety and recommitment to Christ with a ceremony of re-baptism.

Claudia is sixty-two. Wounded in a bitter divorce eight years ago, her church offered her little but awkwardness and shame. She left. Now, invited to a small group through a friend in her apartment complex, she is ready to return to active membership in a different congregation. She, too, comes to her pastor and asks for a ceremony of blessing and incorporation.

honor these special requests and to remind the entire congregation of the need to come to the font for conversion again and again.

On those special days, the normal prayers can be augmented in appropriate ways, providing more substantive celebrations fitting for more significant transitions. For instance, Jim might wish to come forward and, at the font, give the congregation a brief testimony of his bondage and the freedom he now knows in Christ. He can ask them for forgiveness and for blessing. He can make renunciations and affirmations, promise-making to indicate his intention to turn from his old life and towards a new one. Likewise, Claudia may wish to be prayed over by the elders, who would lay hands on her, commission her to ministry in the church's ESL program, and make the mark of the cross on her forehead with fragrant oil.

Special requests then become excellent opportunities for focused pastoral ministry by congregants eager to learn and open to teaching. Mary, for instance, comes to the pastor in June, but her baptismal anniversary is in November: a four-month window for a mini-catechumenate. She has at least four months in which she and her pastor can process her summer mission experience, four months to explore the implications of a recommitment to Christ, four months to add thicker logs of Christian discipline and community to the flame of renewal lit in the Yucatan.

Some are already wondering, though: what about those who do not know the dates of their baptisms? Many will be able to identify (or estimate) their dates with sufficient precision. But for others, there are two options:

1) Select the day eight days after one's birthday—echoing the date on which Jewish males were circumcised—the date on which members of the Jewish covenant community came to be marked by God.

2) Select as the baptismal anniversary the date of conception. No need for research. Just go backwards nine months from the birthday. This has resonance in the church's history, since celebrations for saints happened not on the dates of their birth (which folks often did not know, and did not mark), but on the dates of their death (and hence rebirth to eternal life). It was thought that the day a saint died was the same date on which that person was conceived.[52]

One further benefit of a regular practice like this is its emphasis on the mission of the church. Many denominations are wrestling with the roles

---

52. This is one theory for why we celebrate Christ's birth on December 25th. Some calculate that in the year Jesus died—the day before Passover, Good Friday, was the 25th of March. A little bit of nine-month math, and we arrive at December 25 as Christ's birthday. See McGowan, "How December 25 Became Christmas."

and purposes of ordained offices and newfangled extensions of them—"commissioned pastors," "lay preachers," etc. How wonderful, then, to be persistently reminded of the common calling all Christians share, by virtue of their baptisms, to be more missional—to look for God's work in the world and to join in that redemptive and reconciling action. Another benefit: featuring the font in worship is a way to mark a clear distinction between the church and the world out of which the church has been called. To highlight the boundary between life in Christ and life outside is not to demean or diminish one group as outsiders, but to invite them to jump in the pool where Christians have found life abundant.

I am convinced that regular and varied celebration of this sort could go a long way toward helping us to experience and understand the richness of meaning embodied in the sacrament, to see God's ongoing work more clearly, and to affirm our need for a faith-filled return to the living water again and again.

WORSHIP EVALUATION

The following section offers a final suggestion for ecclesial practice, emerging from some of von Allmen's insights and, in some ways, from his methodology as well. The issue in view is the way in which a community of believers articulates and deploys its standards for excellence in worship.

In a summative assignment for a worship class, a student we will call "Josh" at Western Theological Seminary recently reflected on the questions with which he began the semester:

> Some of the primary motivating questions I had coming into the course were questions regarding what constitutes "gathered worship" (i.e., how do we know if "church" happened? If three people from my church share a meal and talk about how much they love Jesus at the meal, is that a "worship service"? What if they look at the Bible, too?). . . . I also still wonder sometimes what constitutes valid worship practices. For example, a few weeks ago, my church used birthday cake instead of bread for communion.

One can hear in this student's musings two common impulses, impulses in tension with one another. On the one hand, he wants to know what is *correct*, what is the *valid* way to do worship, to shape a communion liturgy, or conduct baptism or a funeral. He wants to get the rites right. But one may also hear, more subtly, an impulse to subvert received tradition, to resist authority, to see what the freedoms we have in Christ look like when applied to worship. Notice that Josh does not actually ask the authority figure assessing his work whether the birthday cake communion was an infraction of some law of fraction.

The tension between law and liberty is not foreign to Jean-Jacques von Allmen. Grounded in relational and liturgical unity as well as temporal and spatial catholicity, von Allmen writes that among the "norms of liturgical expression" include first a "respect for tradition (which is part of the communal character of the Biblical cult of which we have just been speaking). When we perform Christian worship, we are part of the Church of all places and all times, and this community binds us."[53]

It is important to remember that this "respect for tradition" as well as the mandate and freedom to enculturate worship in the *hic et nunc* are, for von Allmen, "derivative" norms. That is to say, they emerge only subsequent to the primary norm for worship, which is foundational apostolicity, or "fidelity to the Bible." This includes a handful of measures: that worship take place in Christ's name and to meet him with the intention of being Christian worship, that it engages the apostolic teaching about Jesus, that it enables the communion of the body of Christ at the table, that it gathers up the prayers of the church to offer them to God, and that it be a people sharing a common life.[54]

But to respect tradition, von Allmen continues, "implies to be free with regard to it." Here is another norm of liturgical expression in some tension with the first. Because the church is an eschatological people, the Kingdom is always bursting forth in new ways, even in the structure of worship. Indeed, the church "has the right and even the duty of expressing itself by prayers, hymns, and symbols which ever anew are inspired by the Spirit of God."[55]

---

53. von Allmen, *Worship*, 97.

54. von Allmen, *Worship*, 96.

55. von Allmen, *Worship*, 99. Later, von Allmen concludes: "The form of worship is both strict and free. Strict, because it is a question of Christian worship; free, because liturgy is an "eschatological game" (Romano Guardini), the finest of all the games that men are invited to play on earth. But a game, in order not to degenerate into license, an orgy or a scuffle, needs to be played with disciplined liberty. . . . The limits of such liberty always viewed within the framework of the norms and conditions of Christian worship—are those set by the unity of the Church, a unity which, however, does not imply uniformity" (von Allmen, *Worship*, 105).

In the tension between the impulse to conform and the impulse to experiment is a locus of both ecclesial anxiety and of pedagogical promise. Behind both of them is a desire for "good" worship: worship that is both correct and meaningful, worship that is pleasing to God and to us, worship that meets a community's expectations for what worship *should* do and be, while not limiting God's freedom to act outside of those expectations. A goal for any community negotiating this tension is to articulate standards of excellence without needing to appeal to some kind of liturgy police (or deputizing its own officers).

One might summarize the scholarly conversation around the Latin phrase *Lex Orandi, Lex Credendi* by suggesting that a good way to approach the complexities of norming worship practices is to recognize the inter-relationships without demanding their character be defined more precisely than is possible. Rather than simply (and perhaps simplistically) declaring a prayer book or something else as the last word, rather than pursuing the establishment of *orandi* in *credendi* with a nod to *agendi*—or some other configuration of laws—we might strive instead for a rich congruence between what we say we believe and the beliefs embodied in our worship practices.

"Good" worship finds congruence between fundamental theological convictions and practices that express and shape them. To pick one small example, if we believe that God *acts*, then our words in worship, including in our songs, will testify to that action in vivid ways. If we do not so testify, we may find that our congregations are full of people who doubt that God has the ability to will and act in our lives today. When what we mean and what we do in worship are congruent, when they match up, worship is *good*—beautiful, meaningful, and wide open to God's transforming power.

The ecclesial practice suggested by this analysis, then, is to help congregations both *norm* their practice and to *name* it, both descriptively and aspirationally—articulating what they hope worship, by God's grace, might be, what virtues it might exhibit, and what promise it could be expected to fulfill in their lives.

John Witvliet, in his essay "Teaching Worship as a Christian Practice," warns of the danger of a legalistic approach to articulating standards of excellence: "It is fearsome indeed to find a new seminary graduate off to his or her first charge with the message that all the old worship practices there are wrong and need to be fixed."[56] Witvliet argues instead for the use

---

56. Witvliet, "Teaching Worship" 144–45.

of the "rhetoric of wisdom" rather than a "rhetoric of law." He sees this as a way to "reframe discussions about right and wrong, better and worse in ways that appreciate the excellencies of some approaches, but with a sense of contingency of that practice in certain contexts."

One can see this approach in the statement on worship adopted by the newly formed World Communion of Reformed Churches in 2010. There, statements about worship practices and the principles that inform them are articulated not with a "Worship should" or "Worship must," but with a "Wise is the congregation that" or "Blessed is the people of God who . . ."[57]

Such an approach has a number of advantages. Among the most important is that the shift from prescriptive to descriptive helps those engaged in the process to enter into the inner logic of certain choices and practices and to claim and own that logic for themselves. Meanwhile, perhaps surprisingly, they discover new practices or riffs on old practices that pursue an aspirational goal with even greater fittingness for a particular community. So, for instance, the approach is not "you must always pray in a collect form" but "here is a gift—the collect form—that embodies the inner logic of prayer, grounding our intercessions in the revealed character and actions of God. What ways can you lead prayer that do this same thing?" One hears echoes of von Allmen: "If a fine doxology of Christian antiquity is golden, it is a gold coin rather than a gold chain. That is to say, that respect for the traditions of worship does not fetter liturgical expression, but on the contrary, enables us to repeat today in a new way what the Fathers said when they assembled to celebrate the mystery of Christian salvation."[58]

Furthermore, in moving to descriptive, one does not actually lose the prescriptive—it sneaks in the back door. Every attempt to articulate a rich aspirational description is a type of normative statement, but one that is internally motivated rather than externally imposed.

One way to pursue this approach within a particular congregational context is to work together, as a community, to discern and articulate standards of excellence in the form of *descriptive adjectives*—a list that is evocative and generative rather than comprehensive. This is precisely the methodology that von Allmen employs when he describes the *church's* character through its worship. It is, as we have seen, eschatological, nuptial, baptismal, Eucharistic, local, and diaconal.

57. See World Communion of Reformed Churches, "Worshipping the Triune God."
58. von Allmen, *Worship*, 97.

No collection of adjectives will ever fully articulate the norms for excellent practice, of course, and some propositional content may have to be set forth to identify the center of the cluster and as a hedge against misinterpretation. But imagine a cluster of words generated—as was the list below—by a community reflecting on what it considered to be its greatest hopes for worship.

Active	Affective	Awesome
Beautiful	Biblical	Christocentric
Communal	Covenantal	Cross-cultural
Diachronic	Dialogical	Enabling
Energetic	Engaging	Eschatological
Eventful	Expansive	Expectant
Free	Holistic	Honest
Hopeful	Joyful	Majestic
Ordered	Participative	Relational
Reverent	Sacramental	Spirit-directed
Spontaneous	Surprising	Trinitarian

The wisdom gathered here is community-based. There is some transportability from one worshipping community to another, but no two communities would come up with the same lists of adjectives. This reflects the way we have come to understand knowledge in our postmodern era as community-based and not simply objective. Note, too, that this list, once compiled, can be normative in a non-coercive way, vital for deepening praxis: everyone will agree on them. Emerging in a group process, they are *shared* norms that can then guide the critique and shaping of a community's worship, lest critique devolve into power struggles between what one person "likes" over against what another "likes."

Longer lists like the one above might be unwieldy for practical use, but a condensed list can be helpful in keeping a community honest and accountable for what "good worship" is. Consider this one, found in the opening pages of the *Worship Sourcebook*: Biblical, Dialogic, Covenantal, Trinitarian, Hospitable, and Excellent.[59]

Note that the adjective "Biblical" is given a place of privilege. But when the Word is invoked, it is not to stop the conversation cold, but to

59. Steenwyk and Witvliet, *Worship Sourcebook*, 15–16.

invite careful thought. When one encounters arguments by those who wish to norm the church's pattern for Lord's Day services in the worship of the ancient Hebrews in the Tabernacle and Temple, one might now furrow a brow and wonder whether this is the *best* approach for New Testament Christians. Not "correct" or "wrong," but "best."

To provide a bit more texture to simple descriptors, the *Sourcebook* offers amplifying statements for each of its primary adjectives. The one for "Biblical" reads:

> The bible is the source of our knowledge of God and of the world's redemption in Christ. Worship should include prominent readings of Scripture. It should present and depict God's being, character, and actions in ways that are consistent with scriptural teaching. It should obey explicit biblical commands about worship practices, and it should heed scriptural warnings about false and improper worship. Worship should focus its primary attention where the Bible does: on the person and work of Jesus Christ as the Redeemer of all creation and the founder and harbinger of the kingdom of God through the work of the Holy Spirit.[60]

One might add—with, I imagine, von Allmen's blessing—an additional adjective and its gloss: Expectant. The Spirit blows where she will, so we worship with our sails raised, expecting great things of God, and enjoying, rather than engineering, a contagious spiritual energy. When worship is not about how hard we pray, how comprehensively we confess, how beautifully we sing, how much water is used at the Easter Vigil baptism, or how carefully we follow a rulebook. When instead it is about how open we can try to be to the Spirit's power, recognizing that the Spirit can work with forms and patterns, norms and names, but is not *bound* by them—then we can worship with a kind of holy expectancy.

So perhaps one might suggest that Josh's birthday cake communion was not a "valid" celebration of the Lord's Supper, and even by standards of aspirational description and naming, it was probably less than it might have been. Nevertheless, there is, in this approach, a recognition that the Spirit can and does work in less than ideal circumstances, that God is in the salvage business, that Jesus Christ takes all our warbly singing and half-hearted praying and distracted listening and thoughtless communing, and

---

60. Steenwyk and Witvliet, *Worship Sourcebook*, 16.

perfects them all in his perfect priesthood.[61] Then, the worship we offer is much more than just "good."

CONCLUSION

The several worship issues considered in this chapter are not the only troublesome questions in the church today. Norming or evaluating worship practices, adult versus infant baptism, the question of open communion and the challenges raised by a set-apart people, the nature and role of preaching and its relation to sacraments, the best way to order a worship service, and the frequency of communion—these are only a few important and common issues that pastors and worship leaders grapple with in their daily work in the church. I have tried to demonstrate here that each of these issues deserves careful theological consideration and that, in each case, Jean-Jacques von Allmen's work offers relevant and helpful guidance, categories of thought, or at least helpful questions that clarify the issues at hand. I have shown how applying the three abiding themes in von Allmen's work—recapitulation, manifestation, and promise/threat—can generate some practical guidance. More importantly, drawing out the subdivisions and nuances in von Allmen's discussions of the Nicene marks reveals the interrelatedness of those issues and allows a finer grained application to specific issues the church now faces.

Von Allmen's historical moment and his particular gifts—as a mid-twentieth century Reformed ecumenist, equally skilled as a theologian in the study and a pastor in the congregation—uniquely positioned him to become a pioneer in the field of liturgical ecclesiology. Even before that field had a name, von Allmen was creating a legacy of writings that established the usefulness of this approach, not only for his own time but also for ours. My hope is that this study will contribute in some small way to a renewal of interest in von Allmen and in the potential of his work to speak into the church in this generation and in the generations to come.

---

61. See Torrance, *Worship, Community, and the Triune God of Grace.*

Bibliography

Agnew, Mary Barbara. *The Concept of Sacrifice in the Eucharistic Theology of Donald M. Baille, Thomas F. Torrance, and Jean-Jacques von Allmen*. Ann Arbor, MI: Catholic University of America, 1972.

Anderson, Ray. *The Shape of Practical Theology: Empowering Ministry with Theological Praxis*. Downers Grove, IL: InterVarsity, 2001.

Aquinas, Thomas. "Exposition on the Apostle's Creed." In *Catechetical Instructions of St. Thomas*, translated by Joseph B. Collins, 48–53. New York: Wagner, 1939.

Augustine, Aurelius. *The City of God*. Vol. 1–2 of *The Works of Aurelius Augustine, Bishop of Hippo: A New Translation*. Translated by Marcus Dods. Edinburgh: T&T Clark, 1888.

Barot, Madeline, and Adriano Prosperi. *Il movimento ecumenico: il testo de Madeleine Barot e i confronti antologici da O. Cullmann, H. Küng, J.-J. von Allmen, W.A. Visser't Hooft, L. Vischer, Y. Congar, H. Camara, A., Nesti, L. Basso*. Messina-Firenze: G. D'Anna, 1973.

Barth, Karl. *Dogmatics in Outline*. New York: Harper Perennial, 1959.

———. *The Teaching of the Church Regarding Baptism*. London: SCM, 1948.

Berkhof, Hendrikus. *Christian Faith: An Introduction to the Study of the Faith*. Translated by Sierd Woudstra. Revised Edition. Grand Rapids: Eerdmans, 1979.

Bharath, Deepa. "Crystal Cathedral board picks diocese over Chapman." Orange County Register. 17 November 2011. http://www.ocregister.com/news/chapman-327576-cathedral-board.html.

Bobrinski, Boris, et al., eds. *Communio Sanctorum, Mélanges offerts à Jean-Jacques von Allmen*. Genève: Labor Et Fides, 1982.

Bradshaw, Paul F. *Eucharistic Origins*. New York: Oxford University Press, 2004.

———, ed. *The New Dictionary of Liturgy and Worship*. London: SCM, 2002.

Bridel, Claude. "Jean-Jacques von Almen (1917); la passion de unité." In *Herausgegeben von Stephan Leimgruber und Max Schoch, Gegen Die Gottvergessenheit: Schweizer Theologen Im 19. Und 20. Jahrhundert*, 561–75. Basel: Herder, 1990.

Burki, Bruno. "Jean-Jacques von Allmen dans le Mouvement Liturgique." *Studia Liturgica* 16–17 (1986–87) 52–61.

Byars, Ronald P. *The Sacraments in Biblical Perspective*. Louisville: WKJ, 2001.

Calvin, John. "Institutes of the Christian Religion (1559)." In *Calvin: Institutes of the Christian Religion*, translated by John T. McNeill and edited by Ford Lewis Battles. Library of Christian Classics. Louisville: WJK, 1960.

Chan, Simon. *Liturgical Theology: The Church as Worshipping Community*. Downers Grove, IL: InterVarsity, 2006.

Congar, Yves, et al., eds. *Communio Sanctorum: mélanges offerts à Jean-Jacques von Allmen*. Geneva: Editions Labor et Fides, 1982.

Cuminetti, Mario. *Element "cattolici" nella dottrina del minister di alcuni teologi calvinisti contemporanei: J.J. von Allmen, J.L. Leuba, R. Paquier, M. Thurian*. Roma: Libreria editrice dell'Università Gregoriana, 1965.

Davis, Leo Donald, SJ. *The First Seven Ecumenical Councils*. Collegeville, MN: Liturgical, 1990.

Day, David, et al., eds. *A Reader on Preaching: Making Connections*. Aldershot: Ashgate, 2005.

Dix, Dom Gregory. *The Shape of the Liturgy*. New York: Bloomsbury Academic, 2005.

Dulles, Avery Cardinal. *Models of the Church*. Expanded edition. New York: Doubleday, 2002.

Fagerberg, David W. *Theologia Prima: What Is Liturgical Theology?* Second Edition. Chicago: Hillenbrand, 2007.

Fenwick, John R. K., and Bryan D. Spinks. *Worship In Transition: The Liturgical Movement In the Twentieth Century*. New York: Continuum, 1995.

Flannery, Austin, ed. "Dogmatic constitution on the Church: Lumen Gentium." In *Vatican Council II: The Basic Sixteen Documents*, 1–95. Collegeville, MN: Liturgical, 2014.

Florovsky, George. "The Elements of Liturgy in the Orthodox Catholic Church." *One Church* 13.1–2 (1959) 24.

Foley, Edward. *From Age to Age: How Christians Celebrated the Eucharist*. Chicago: LTP, 1991.

Gibbs, Eddie. *ChurchNext: Quantum Changes in How We Do Ministry*. Downers Grove, IL: InterVarsity, 2000.

Grant, Robert M. *Irenaeus of Lyons*. Early Church Fathers. New York: Routledge, 1997.

Greenslade, S. L., ed. *Early Latin Theology: Selections from Tertullian, Cyprian, Ambrose and Jerome*. Library of Christian Classics. Louisville: Westminster, 1956.

Guder, Darrell L. *The Continuing Conversion of the Church*. Grand Rapids: Eerdmans, 2000.

———, ed. *Missional Church: A Vision for the Sending of the Church in North America*. Grand Rapids: Eerdmans, 1998.

Hageman, Howard. *Pulpit & Table*. Eugene, OR: Wipf & Stock, 2004.

Haquin, André. "Les sacrements de l'initiation chrétienne selon le pasteur J.-J. von Allmen." In *Initiation chrétienne et la liturgie*, 135–50. Leuven: Peeters, 2008.

"Heidelberg Catechism." Reformed Church in America. https://www.rca.org/resources/heidelbergcatechism.

Henderson, Earnest F., ed. *Select Historical Documents of the Middle Ages*. London: George Bell and Sons, 1892.

Hilkert, Marcy Catharine. *Naming Grace: Preaching and the Sacramental Imagination*. New York: Bloomsbury Academy, 1997.

Hoffman, Lawrence. "How Ritual Means: Ritual Circumcision in Rabbinic Culture and Today." *Studia Liturgica* 23 (1993) 78–97.

Holmes, Michael W., ed. *The Apostolic Fathers in English*. 3rd edition. Grand Rapids: Baker Academic, 2006.

Hughes, Kathleen, ed. *How Firm a Foundation: Voices of the Early Liturgical Movement*. Chicago: LTP, 1990.

Irwin, Kevin. "Liturgical Theology." In *New Dictionary of Sacramental Worship*, 721–22. Collegeville, MN: Liturgical,1990.

Johnson, Maxwell. *Praying and Believing in Early Christianity: The Interplay between Christian Worship and Doctrine*. Collegeville, MN: Liturgical, 2013.

Johnson, Todd E. "The State of Liturgical Renewal: A Vision Unread." *Liturgy* 26.4 (2011) 1–3.

Kärkkäinen, Veli-Matti. *An Introduction to Ecclesiology*. Downers Grove, IL: InterVarsity, 2002.

Kavanagh, Aidan. *On Liturgical Theology*. New York: Pueblo, 1984

Keble, John, ed. *The Works of that Learned and Judicious Divine, Mr. Richard Hooker: With an Account of His Life and Death by Isaac Walton*. Oxford: Oxford University Press, 1936.

Kilmartin, Edward J. *Christian Liturgy I: Theology*. Kansas City: Sheed & Ward, 1988.

———.*The Eucharist in the West: History and Theology*. Collegeville, MN: Liturgical, 1999.

Küng, Hans. *The Church*. New York: Sheed & Ward, 1967.

Lathrop, Gordon W. *Holy Ground: A Liturgical Cosmology*. Minneapolis: Fortress, 2003.

———. *Holy People: A Liturgical Ecclesiology*. Minneapolis: Fortress, 1999.

———. *Holy Things: A Liturgical Theology*. Minneapolis: Fortress, 1998.

Lathrop, Gordon, and Timothy J. Wengert. *Christian Assembly: Marks of the Church in a Pluralistic Age*. Minneapolis: Augsberg, 2004.

Lemoine, Jacques, "Célébrer le salut:culte chrétien et oecuménisme selon J J von Allmen." *Irénikon* 60.1 (1987) 53.

Long, Tom. *Beyond the Worship Wars: Building Vital and Faithful Worship*. Bethesda: Alban Institute, 2002.

———. "The Distance We Have Traveled: Changing Trends in Preaching." In *A Reader on Preaching*, edited by David Day, Jeff Astley, and Leslie J. Francis, 11–16. Burlington: Ashgate, 2005.

Maddox, Randy. "Practical Theology: a Discipline in Search of a Definition." *Perspectives in Religious Studies* 18 (1991) 159–69.

Mateos, Fr. Juan."The Message of Jesus." Translated by Kathleen England. *Sojourners* 6.7 (1977) 8–16.

McGowan, Andrew. "How December 25 Became Christmas." Bible History Daily. 3 December 2017. https://www.biblicalarchaeology.org/daily/biblical-topics/new-testament/how-december-25-became-christmas.

———. "Rethinking Eucharistic Origins." *Pacifica* 23 (2010) 173–91.

Meyendorff, John. "The Orthodox Concept of the Church." *St. Vladimir's Quarterly* 6.2 (1962) 59–72.

Mitchell, Nathan. "The Amen Corner: Being Good and Being Beautiful." *Worship* 74.6 (2000) 557–58.

———. "Liturgy and Ecclesiology." In *Fundamental Liturgy*, edited by Anscar Chupungco. Vol. 2. Collegeville, MN: Liturgical, 1998.

Moltmann, Jurgen. *The Church in the Power of the Spirit: a Contribution to Messianic Ecclesiology*. Translated by Margaret Kohl. New York: Harper & Row, 1977.

Montmollin, Michael. "Jean-Jacques von Allmen, théologien et professeur (1917–1994)." In *Biographies Neuchâteloises*, 315–18. Vol 5. Hauterive: Editions Gilles Attinger, 1996.

Newbigin, Lesslie. *The Household of God*. London: SCM, 1953.

Old, Hughes Oliphant. *Holy Communion in the Piety of the Reformed Church*. Dallas, GA: Tolle Lege, 2014.

———. "Reminiscences and Reflections Concerning Jean-Jacques von Allmen." Unpublished correspondence. 2009.

Pecklers, Keith. *An Unread Vision: The Liturgical Movement in the United States of America 1926–1955*. Collegeville, MN: Liturgical, 1998.

Pelikan, Jaroslav. *The Christian Tradition: A History of the Development of Doctrine*. Vol. 5. Chicago: University of Chicago, 1989.

Ploeger, Matthijs. *Celebrating Church: Ecumenical Contributions to a Liturgical Ecclesiology*. Netherlands Studies in Ritual and Liturgy 7. Groningen: Institut voor Liturgiewetenschap, 2008.

Presbyterian Church. "Invitation to Christ: A Guide to Sacramental Practices." Louisville: Presbyterian Church (USA), 2006. https://www.pcusa.org/site_media/media/uploads/sacraments/pdfs/invitationtochrist.pdf.

Prusak, Bernard P. *The Church Unfinished: Ecclesiology Through the Centuries*. Mahwah, NJ: Paulist, 2004.

Reformed Church in America. "Directory for Worship." Liturgy of the RCA. https://www.rca.org/resources/directory-worship.

Richardson, Cyril, ed. *Early Christian Fathers*. Library of Christian Classics. Louisville: WJK, 1953.

Rienstra, Ron. "Good Worship: Articulating Standards of Excellence in Worship without Becoming the Liturgy Police." *Liturgy* 29.2 (2014) 52–58.

Roberts, Alexander, and James Donaldson, eds. *The Ante-Nicene Fathers: Translations of the Writings of the Fathers down to AD 325*. Vol. 2. Edinburgh: T&T Clark, 1866–72.

Robinson, James H. *Readings in European History*. Boston: Ginn & Co., 1904.

Saliers, Don. "Review of Holy People: A Liturgical Ecclesiology, by Gordon Lathrop." *Cross Accent: A Journal of the Association of Lutheran Church Musicians* 8.3 (2000) 30.

———. *Worship as Theology: Foretaste of Glory Divine*. Nashville: Abingdon, 1994.

Santa Cruz, Nicole, Ruben Vives, and Mitchell Landsberg. "O.C. Catholic diocese to buy bankrupt Crystal Cathedral." Los Angeles Times. 18 November 2011. http://articles.latimes.com/2011/nov/18/local/la-me-crystal-cathedral-20111118.

Satterlee, Craig Alan, and Lester Ruth. *Creative Preaching On the Sacraments*. Nashville, TN: Discipleship Resources, 2001. Kindle Edition.

Schmemann, Alexander. *Introduction to Liturgical Theology*. Translated Asheleigh E. Moorhouse. Crestwood, NY: St. Vladimir, 1986.

———. "Theology and Liturgy." *Greek Orthodox Theological Review* 17.1 (1972) 94.

Schmit, Clayton J. *Sent and Gathered: a Worship Manual for the Missional Church*. Grand Rapids: Baker Academic, 2009.

"The Second Helvetic Confession." Christian Classics Ethereal Library. https://www.ccel.org/creeds/helvetic.htm.

Second Vatican Council. "Constitution on the Sacred Liturgy: *Sacrosanctum Concilium* (4 December 1963)." In *The Sixteen Documents of Vatican II*, edited by Marianne L. Trouve, 47–83. Boston: Pauline Books, 1999.

Senn, Frank. *Christian Liturgy*. Minneapolis: Fortress, 1997.

———. "Worship, Doctrine, and Life: Liturgical Theology, Theologies of Worship, and Doxological Theology." *Currents in Theology and Mission* 9 (1982) 11–13.

Smith, James K. A. *Imagining the Kingdom: How Worship Works*. Cultural Liturgies. Grand Rapids: Baker Academic, 2013.

Spinks, Bryan D., ed. *The Place of Christ in Liturgical Prayer: Trinity, Christology, and Liturgical Theology.* Collegeville, MN: Liturgical, 2008.

Steenwyk, Carrie Titcombe, and John D. Witvliet, eds. *The Worship Sourcebook.* 2nd edition. Grand Rapids: Baker, 2013.

Stone, Bryan P. *A Reader in Ecclesiology.* Burlington, VT: Ashgate, 2012.

Taxin, Amy. "Can Crystal Cathedral survive without its church?" Bloomberg BusinessWeek. 17 November 2011. http://www.businessweek.com/ap/financialnews/D9R2J42O1.htm.

———. "Crystal Cathedral sees risky future without church." San Diego Union-Tribune. 18 November 2011. http://www.sandiegouniontribune.com/sdut-crystal-cathedral-sees-risky-future-without-church-2011nov18-story.html.

Torrance, James B. *Worship, Community, and the Triune God of Grace.* Downers Grove, IL: InterVarsity, 1997.

Townsend, Todd. *The Sacramentality of Preaching.* New York: Peter Lang, 2009.

Tuzik, Robert L., ed. *How Firm a Foundation: Leaders of the Liturgical Movement.* Chicago: Liturgy Training Publications, 1990.

Van Gelder, Craig. *The Essence of the Church: A Community Created by the Spirit.* Grand Rapids: Baker, 2000.

Vander Zee, Leonard. *Christ, Baptism, and the Lord's Supper: Recovering the Sacraments for Evangelical Worship.* Downers Grove, IL: InterVarsity, 2004.

Vogel, Dwight, ed. *Primary Sources of Liturgical Theology.* Collegeville, MN: Liturgical, 2000.

von Allmen, Jean-Jacques. *Célébrer le Salut, Doctrine et pratique du cute chrétien.* Genève: Labor et Fides. Paris: Cerf, 1984.

———. "The Continuity of the Church According to Reformed Teaching." *Journal of Ecumenical Studies* 1.3 (1964) 424–44.

———. *Essai sur le reps du Seigneur.* Neuchâtel: Delachaux et Niestlé, 1966.

———. "The Forgiveness of Sins as a Sacrament in the Reformed Tradition." In *Sacramental Reconciliation,* translated by Robin Baird-Smith and edited by Edward Schillebeeckx, 112–119. New York: Herder and Herder, 1971.

———. "L'actualité de J.F. Ostervald (1663–1747), second réformateur de l'Eglise neuchâteloise." Neuchâtel: Verbum Caro, 1948.

———. *L'Eglise et ses fonctions d'après Jean-Frédéric Ostervald.* Neuchâtel: Delachaux & Niestlé, 1948.

———. "La primauté de l'Eglise de Pierre et du Paul: remarques d'un Protestant." In *Cahiers oecuméniques 10, Editions Universitaires/Friborg.* Paris: Cerf, 1977.

———. *Le Saint Ministère selon la conviction et la volonté des Réformés du XVIe siècle, Bibliothèque Théologique.* Neuchâtel: Delachaux & Niestlé, 1968.

———. "Les Conditions d'une intercommunion acceptable: repose d'un réformé." *Concilium: revue internationale de théologie* 44 (1969) 13–20.

———. "Les Marques De L'Église." *Revue De Théologie Et De Philosophie* 113.2 (1982) 97–107.

———. *The Lord's Supper.* Ecumenical Studies in Worship 19. London: Lutterworth, 1968.

———. "On the Theological Meaning of Common Prayer." *Studia Liturgica* 10.3–4 (1974) 129.

———. "Ordination: A Sacrament? a Protestant Reply." *Concilium: revue internationale de théologie* 74 (1972) 40–48.

———. "Pastorale du baptême." In *Cahiers oecuméniques 12, Editions Universitaires/ Fribourg*. Paris: Cerf, 1978. Upublished English translation by Rita Selles.

———. *Preaching and Congregation*. Ecumenical Studies in Worship 10. Translated by B. L. Nichols. Richmond: John Knox, 1962.

———. *Prophétisme sacramentel: neuf etudes sur le renouveau et l'unité de l'Eglise*. Neuchâtel:Delachaux & Niestlé, 1964.

———. "Réflexions d'un Protestant sur le pédobaptisme généralisé." *La Maison-Dieu, revue de pastoral liturgique, Paris* 89 (1967) 66–86.

———. "The Theological Frame of a Liturgical Renewal." *Church Quarterly* 2 (1969–70) 8–23.

———. *Une réforme dans l'Eglise: Possibilité, critères, acteurs, étapes. Leçons données dans la chaire Dom Lambert Beauduin, à l'Univ. de Louvain, en janvier et février, 1970*. Gembloux: Duculot, 1971.

———. *Vocabularie Biblique*. Paris: Delachaux & Niestlé, 1954.

———. *Vocabulary of the Bible*. London: Lutterworth, 1958.

———. *Worship: Its Theology & Practice*. Translated by Harold Knight and W. Fletcher Fleet. London: Lutterworth, 1965.

Wainwright, Geoffrey. *Doxology: The Praise of God in Worship, Doctrine, and Life*. London: Epworth, 1980.

———. *Worship with One Accord: Where Liturgy and Ecumenism Embrace*. New York: Oxford University Press, 1997.

Wainwright, Geoffrey, and Karen B. Westerfield Tucker, eds. *The Oxford History of Christian Worship*. New York: Oxford University Press, 2006.

Warren, Rick. *The Purpose Driven Church*. Grand Rapids: Zondervan, 2011.

Wasserman, Barry. "Letters: Crystal Cathedral sold to the second-highest bidder?" Orange County Register. 21 November 2011. http://www.ocregister.com/opinion/-328099—. html.

Webber, Robert. *Ancient-Future Evangelism*. Grand Rapids: Baker, 2003.

———. *Common Roots: The Original Call to an Ancient-Future Faith*. Grand Rapids: Zondervan, 1978.

Webber, Robert, et al. "The Chicago Call: An Appeal to Evangelicals." Per-Fidem. http:// www.per-fidem.org/bookshelf/chicagocall.html.

White, James F. *The Cambridge Movement: the Ecclesiologists and the Gothic Revival*. Revised edition. Cambridge: Cambridge University, 1979.

———. *Protestant Worship: Traditions in Transition*. Louisville: Westminster John Knox, 1989.

———. *Roman Catholic Worship: Trent to Today*. 2nd edition. Collegeville, MN: Pueblo, 2004.

Wilson, Paul Scott. *The Four Pages of a Sermon: A Guide to Biblical Preaching*. Nashville: Abingdon, 1999.

Witvliet, John. "Teaching Worship as a Christian Practice." In *For Life Abundant: Practical Theology, Theological Education, and Christian Ministry*, edited by Dorothy Bass and Craig Dykstra, 144–45. Grand Rapids: Eerdmans, 2006.

Wolterstorff, Nicholas. *The God We Worship: An Exploration of Liturgical Theology*. Grand Rapids: Eerdmans, 2015.

World Communion of Reformed Churches. "Worshipping the Triune God: Receiving and Sharing Christian Wisdom Across Continents and Centuries." Calvin Institute of Christian Worship. 7 January 2011. http://www.calvin.edu/cicw/resources/

Worshiping%20the%20Triune%20God%20PDFs/WorshipingTheTriuneGod-English.pdf.

World Council of Churches. *The Nature and Mission of the Church: A Stage on the Way to a Common Statement*. Faith and Order 198. Geneva: World Council of Churches, 2005.

Wright, N. T. *The Meal Jesus Gave Us*. Louisville: WJK, 2002.

Zwingli, Huldrych. "An Exposition of the Faith." In *Zwingli and Bullinger*, edited by G. W. Bromiley, 245–279. Library of Christian Classics. Philadelphia: Westminster, 1953.

Made in the USA
Lexington, KY
06 March 2019